Daily Services
Morning & Evening Prayer

from
A Prayer Book for Australia

**BROUGHTON
PUBLISHING**

Published by Broughton Publishing
Your National Anglican Publisher
32 Glenvale Crescent
Mulgrave Victoria 3170
Australia

www.broughtonpublishing.com.au

Notice The inclusion of a psalm in each service means that the pagination does not correspond with *A Prayer Book for Australia*.

First printing 2006

National Library of Australia Cataloguing-in-Publication data -

Daily Services

ISBN 978-1-9208922-1-0

1. Anglican Church of Australia – Prayer-books and devotions. 2. Anglican Church of Australia – Liturgy Anglican Church of Australia - Liturgical Commission

264.030994

Editor Charles Sherlock
Cover design David Constable
Cover photo Bill Thomas IMAGEN

Printed in China

Broughton Publishing uses paper made from wood pulp of managed forests, thereby renewing natural resources.

Contents

A note from the Liturgy Commission
of the General Synod of the Anglican Church of Australia

The Daily Services in *A Prayer Book for Australia (1995)*, themselves based on those in *An Australian Prayer Book* (1977), have been taken up widely in the Anglican Church of Australia. In order for them to be used, however, a copy of the Sunday or full edition of *APBA* is needed, as well as a Bible.

Anglican Defence Force chaplains asked that the Daily Services in *APBA* be issued for use in the field. The Liturgy Commission believes that others may find such a booklet helpful, and has therefore prepared this version, in which a psalm is printed within each service. 'Prayer at the End of the Day', and a wide selection of Prayers, Thanksgivings and Blessings from *APBA*, and the weekday collects, are also included.

NB: the printing of a psalm in each service means that the pagination in this booklet does not follow that of *APBA*.

Sunday Morning

1   This is the day which the Lord has made.
    We will rejoice and be glad in it.

Psalm 118.24

Glory to God; Father, Son and Holy Spirit:
    as in the beginning, so now, and for ever. Amen.

2   *The Opening Canticle, A Song of Triumph (Venite)*

O come, let us sing out to the Lord:
  let us shout in triumph to the rock of our salvation.

Let us come before his face with thanksgiving:
  and cry out to him joyfully in psalms.

For the Lord is a great God:
  and a great king above all gods.

In his hand are the depths of the earth:
  and the peaks of the mountains are his also.

The sea is his and he made it:
  his hands moulded dry land.

Come, let us worship and bow down:
  and kneel before the Lord our maker.

For he is the Lord our God:
  we are his people and the sheep of his pasture.

Today if only you would hear his voice:
  'Do not harden your hearts as Israel did in the wilderness;

'When your forebears tested me:
  put me to proof though they had seen my works.

'Forty years long I loathed that generation and said:
  "It is a people who err in their hearts,
  for they have not known my ways';

'Of whom I swore in my wrath:
  "They shall never enter my rest."'

Psalm 95

> *or the Easter Anthems (Saturday evening ¶ 7) may be used during the Easter season.*

3   *The Opening Prayer*

The night has passed and the day lies open before us;
let us pray with one heart and mind.

> *Silence may be kept.*

As we rejoice in the gift of this new day,
so may the light of your presence, O God,
set our hearts on fire with love for you;
now and for ever. **Amen.**

> *A pause for self-examination, the Confession and Absolution (see Note 1) may be used here.*

4   *The Psalms as appointed, or* **Psalm 98:**

1 O sing to the Lord a new song:
    for he has done marvellous things;

2 His right hand and his holy arm:
    they have got him the victory.

3 The Lord has made known his salvation:
    he has revealed his just deliverance
        in the sight of the nations.

4 He has remembered his mercy and faithfulness
        toward the house of Israel:
    and all the ends of the earth have seen
        the salvation of our God.

5 Shout with joy to the Lord, all the earth:
    break into singing and make melody.

6 Make melody to the Lord upon the harp:
    upon the harp and with the sounds of praise.

7 With trumpets and with horns:
  cry out in triumph before the Lord, the king.

8 Let the sea roar, and all that fills it:
  the good earth and those who live upon it.

9 Let the rivers clap their hands:
  and let the mountains ring out together before the Lord;

10 For he comes to judge the earth:
  he shall judge the world with righteousness,
    and the peoples with equity.

A pause is observed.

5   *At the end of the (last) pause there may follow*

Lord God, whose blessed Son rose in triumph and set us free: grant us the fullness of life he promised us, that through the Holy Spirit our hearts may possess him whom our eyes cannot see, the same Jesus Christ our Lord. **Amen.**

6   *One or two Readings from the Bible as appointed.*

     The readings may be followed by silence for reflection, a hymn or

May your word live in us
  and bear much fruit to your glory.

7   *The Canticle, The Song of Zechariah (Benedictus)*

Blessed be the Lord, the God of Israel:
  who has come to his people and set them free.

The Lord has raised up for us a mighty Saviour:
  born of the house of his servant David.

Through the holy prophets, God promised of old:
  to save us from our enemies,
    from the hands of all who hate us,

To show mercy to our forebears:
  and to remember his holy covenant.

This was the oath God swore to our father Abraham:
  to set us free from the hands of our enemies,

Free to worship him without fear:
   holy and righteous before him, all the days of our life.

And you, child, shall be called the prophet of the Most High:
   for you will go before the Lord to prepare his way,

To give his people knowledge of salvation:
   by the forgiveness of their sins.

In the tender compassion of our God:
   the dawn from on high shall break upon us,

To shine on those who dwell in darkness
   and the shadow of death:
   and to guide our feet into the way of peace.

Luke 1.68-79

8   *The Apostles' Creed may be said.*

I believe in God, the Father almighty,
   creator of heaven and earth.

I believe in Jesus Christ, God's only Son, our Lord,
   who was conceived by the Holy Spirit,
   born of the virgin Mary,
   suffered under Pontius Pilate,
   was crucified, died, and was buried;
   he descended to the dead.
   On the third day he rose from the dead;
   he ascended into heaven,
   and is seated at the right hand of the Father;
   from there he will come to judge
      the living and the dead.

I believe in the Holy Spirit,
   the holy catholic Church,
   the communion of saints,
   the forgiveness of sins,
   the resurrection of the body,
   and the life everlasting. Amen.

9   *The Prayers*

Lord have mercy.
Christ have mercy.
Lord have mercy.

**Our Father in heaven,
hallowed be your name,
your kingdom come,
your will be done,
    on earth as in heaven.
Give us today our daily bread.
Forgive us our sins
    as we forgive those who sin against us.
Save us from the time of trial
    and deliver us from evil.
For the kingdom, the power, and the glory are yours
now and for ever. Amen.**

10   *The Collect of the Day*

11   *Intercessions and Thanksgivings may be made according to local custom and need.*

12   *The Morning Collect*

Eternal God and Father, by whose power we are created and by whose love we are redeemed; guide and strengthen us by your Spirit, that we may give ourselves to your service, and live this day in love to one another and to you; through Jesus Christ our Lord. **Amen.**

13   The Lord be with you.
And also with you.
Let us praise the Lord.
Thanks be to God.

The grace of the Lord Jesus Christ, and the love of God, and the fellowship of the Holy Spirit, be with us all evermore.
Amen.   2 Corinthians 13.14

Sunday Evening

1   Grace, mercy and peace,
      from God the Father, and Jesus Christ our Lord.

1 Timothy 1.2

      Glory to God; Father, Son and Holy Spirit:
      as in the beginning, so now, and for ever. Amen.

2   *The Opening Canticle, The Praise of God's Servants*

      Come now, praise the Lord, all you servants of the Lord:
      you that stand by night in the house of the Lord.

      Lift up your hands in the holy place and praise the Lord:
      May the Lord bless you from Zion,
      the Lord who made heaven and earth.

Psalm 134

3   *The Opening Prayer*

      The day is now past and the night is at hand.
      Let us pray with one heart and mind.

      Silence may be kept.

      Father of lights, receive the prayer and praise we offer you
as our evening sacrifice; make us a light for all the world,
delivered by your goodness from all the works of darkness;
through Jesus Christ your Son our Lord. **Amen.**

      *A pause for self-examination, the Confession and Absolution (see
Note 1) may be used here.*

4   *The Psalms as appointed, or* **Psalm 148**:

      1 Praise the Lord, praise the Lord from heaven:
        O praise him in the heights.

      2 Praise him, all his angels:
        O praise him, all his host.

      3 Praise him, sun and moon:
        praise him, all you stars of light.

4 Praise him, you highest heaven:
    and you waters that are above the heavens.

5 Let them praise the name of the Lord:
    for he commanded and they were made.

6 He established them for ever and ever:
    he made an ordinance which shall not pass away.

7 O praise the Lord from the earth:
    praise him, you sea-monsters and all deeps;

8 Fire and hail, mist and snow:
    and storm-wind fulfilling his command;

9 Mountains and all hills:
    fruit trees and all cedars;

10 Beasts of the wild, and all cattle:
    creeping things and winged birds;

11 Kings of the earth, and all peoples:
    princes, and all rulers of the world;

12 Young men and maidens:
    old folk and children together.

13 Let them praise the name of the Lord:
    for his name alone is exalted.

14 His glory is above earth and heaven:
    and he has lifted high the horn of his people.

15 Therefore he is the praise of all his servants:
    of the children of Israel, a people that is near him.
        Praise the Lord.

5.   *A pause is observed, after which there may follow*

Lord of life, by the power of your resurrection, deliver us from all selfishness and bring us to the fullness of your joy; for you live and reign with the Father and the Holy Spirit, now and for ever. **Amen.**

6   *One or two Readings from the Bible as appointed.*

        The readings may be followed by silence for reflection, a hymn, or

May your word live in us
and bear much fruit to your glory.

7   *The Canticle, The Song of Mary (Magnificat)*

My soul proclaims the greatness of the Lord:
  my spirit rejoices in God my Saviour,

Who has looked with favour on his lowly servant:
  from this day all generations will call me blessed;

The Almighty has done great things for me:
  and holy is his name.

God has mercy on those who fear him:
  from generation to generation.

The Lord has shown strength with his arm:
  and scattered the proud in their conceit,

Casting down the mighty from their thrones:
  and lifting up the lowly.

God has filled the hungry with good things:
  and sent the rich away empty.

He has come to the aid of his servant Israel:
  to remember the promise of mercy,

The promise made to our forebears:
  to Abraham and his children for ever.

Luke 1.46–55

8   *The Apostles' Creed may be said (Sunday morning ¶ 8).*

9   *The Prayers*

Lord have mercy.
Christ have mercy.
Lord have mercy.

10   *The Lord's Prayer*

        The Collect of the Day

11   *Intercessions and Thanksgivings may be made according to local custom and need.*

12   *The Evening Collect*

Be present, merciful God, and protect us through the hours of this night: that we, who are wearied by the changes and chances of this fleeting world, may rest on your eternal changelessness; through Jesus Christ our Lord. **Amen.**

13   The Lord be with you.
        And also with you.
        Let us praise the Lord.
        Thanks be to God.

May the God of peace, who brought again from the dead our Lord Jesus, equip us with everything good that we may do his will, to whom be glory for ever. **Amen.**

see Hebrews 13.20, 21

Monday Morning

1   God's love has been poured into our hearts,
through the Holy Spirit who has been given to us.

Romans 5.5

Glory to God; Father, Son and Holy Spirit:
as in the beginning, so now, and for ever. Amen.

2   *The Opening Canticle, a Song of God's Marvellous Acts*

I will sing a new hymn to my God:
O Lord you are great and marvellous,
you are marvellous in your strength invincible.

Let the whole creation serve you:
for you spoke and all things came to be;

You sent out your Spirit and it formed them:
no one can resist your voice.

Mountains and seas are stirred to their depths:
rocks melt like wax at your presence;

But to those who revere you:
you still show mercy.

Judith 16.13–15

3   *The Opening Prayer*

The night has passed and the day lies open before us;
let us pray with one heart and mind.

Silence may be kept.

As we rejoice in the gift of this new day,
so may the light of your presence, O God,
set our hearts on fire with love for you;
now and for ever. **Amen.**

A pause for self-examination, the Confession and Absolution (see Note 1) may be used here.

The Psalms as appointed, or **Psalm 1**:

1 Blessed are they who have not walked in the counsel of
   the ungodly:
   nor followed the way of sinners,
      nor taken their seat amongst the scornful.

2 But their delight is in the law of the Lord:
   and on that law will they ponder day and night.

3 They are like trees planted beside streams of water:
   that yield their fruit in due season.

4 Their leaves also shall not wither:
   and look, whatever they do, it shall prosper.

5 As for the ungodly, it is not so with them:
   they are like the chaff which the wind scatters.

6 Therefore the ungodly shall not stand up at the judgement:
   nor sinners in the congregation of the righteous.

7 For the Lord cares for the way of the righteous:
   but the way of the ungodly shall perish.

5 *A pause is observed, after which there may follow*

Creator Spirit, Advocate promised by our Lord Jesus:
increase our faith and help us to walk in the light of your
presence, to the glory of God the Father; through Jesus
Christ our Lord. **Amen.**

6 *One or two Readings from the Bible as appointed.*

   The readings may be followed by silence for reflection, a hymn or

May your word live in us
   and bear much fruit to your glory.

7 *The Canticle, A Song of Isaiah*

'Behold, God is my salvation:
   I will trust and will not be afraid;

'For the Lord God is my strength and my song:
   and has become my salvation.

With joy you will draw water:
from the wells of salvation.

On that day you will say:
'Give thanks to the Lord, call upon his name;

'Make known his deeds among the nations:
proclaim that his name is exalted.

'Sing God's praises, who has triumphed gloriously:
let this be known in all the world.

'Shout and sing for joy, you that dwell in Zion:
for great in your midst is the Holy One of Israel.'

Isaiah 12.2–6

8   *The Apostles' Creed may be said (Sunday morning ¶ 8).*

9   *The Prayers*

Lord have mercy.
Christ have mercy.
Lord have mercy.

10   *The Lord's Prayer and the Collect of the Day*

11   *Intercessions and Thanksgivings, according to local custom.*

12   *The Morning Collect*

Eternal God and Father, by whose power we are created and by whose love we are redeemed: guide and strengthen us by your Spirit, that we may give ourselves to your service, and live this day in love to one another and to you; through Jesus Christ our Lord. **Amen.**

13   The Lord be with you.
And also with you.
Let us praise the Lord.
Thanks be to God.

God did not give us a spirit of cowardice but a spirit of power and of love and of self-discipline. May we rekindle the gift of God within us. **Amen.**   see 2 Timothy 1.6–7

Monday Evening

1   May the God of hope fill us with all joy and peace in believing,
    so that by the power of the Holy Spirit
    we may abound in hope.

Romans 15.13

Glory to God; Father, Son and Holy Spirit:
    as in the beginning, so now, and for ever. Amen.

2   *The Opening Canticle, A Song of Hope*

The spirit of the Lord God is upon me:
   because the Lord has anointed me
   to bring good tidings to the afflicted.

The Lord has sent me to bind up the broken-hearted:
   to proclaim liberty for the captives,
   and release for those in prison,

To comfort all who mourn:
   to bestow on them a crown of beauty instead of ashes,

The oil of gladness instead of mourning:
   a garment of splendour for the heavy heart.

They shall be called trees of righteousness:
   planted for the glory of the Lord.

Isaiah 61.1–3

3   *The Opening Prayer*

The day is now past and the night is at hand.
Let us pray with one heart and mind.

    Silence may be kept.

Father of lights, receive the prayer and praise we offer you as our evening sacrifice; make us a light for all the world, delivered by your goodness from all the works of darkness; through Jesus Christ your Son our Lord. **Amen.**

    A pause for self-examination, the Confession and Absolution (see Note 1) may be used here.

4	*The Psalms as appointed, or* **Psalm 24**

1 The earth is the Lord's and all that is in it:
    the compass of the world and those who dwell therein.

2 For he has founded it upon the seas:
    and established it upon the waters.

3 Who shall ascend the hill of the Lord:
    or who shall stand in his holy place?

4 Those who have clean hands and a pure heart:
    who have not set their soul upon idols,
        nor sworn their oath to a lie.

5 They shall receive blessing from the Lord:
    and recompense from the God of their salvation.

6 Of such a kind as this are those who seek him:
    those who seek your face, O God of Jacob.

7 *Lift up your heads, O you gates,*
        and be lifted up, you everlasting doors:
    and the King of glory shall come in.

10 Who is the King of glory?:
    the Lord of hosts, he is the King of glory.

5	*A pause is observed, after which there may follow*

God who wonderfully created us and even more wonderfully restored our humanity: strengthen us by your Holy
Spirit to triumph over suffering and death, and grant us
eternal joy; through Jesus Christ our Lord. **Amen.**

6	*One or two Readings from the Bible as appointed.*

	The readings may be followed by silence for reflection, a hymn, or

May your word live in us
    and bear much fruit to your glory.

7	*The Canticle, A Song of God's Children*

In Christ Jesus, the life-giving law of the Spirit:
    has set us free from the law of sin and death.

All who are led by the Spirit of God are children of God:
it is the Spirit that enables us to cry, 'Abba!' Father.

The Spirit bears witness that we are God's children:
and if God's children, then heirs of God.

We are heirs of God and fellow-heirs with Christ:
If we share his sufferings now
we shall be glorified with him hereafter.

These sufferings that we now endure:
are not worth comparing
with the glory that shall be revealed.

For the creation waits with eager longing:
for the revealing of the children of God.

Romans 8.2, 14, 15b–19

8   *The Prayers*

Lord have mercy.
Christ have mercy.
Lord have mercy.

9   *The Lord's Prayer and the Collect of the Day*

10   *Intercessions and Thanksgivings may be made according to local custom and need.*

11   *The Evening Collect*

Lighten our darkness, Lord, we pray: and in your great mercy defend us from all perils and dangers of this night; for the love of your only Son our Saviour Jesus Christ. **Amen.**

12   The Lord be with you.
And also with you.
Let us praise the Lord.
Thanks be to God.

Since we are surrounded by so great a cloud of witnesses, let us run with perseverance the race that is set before us, looking to Jesus the pioneer and perfecter of our faith **Amen.**

Hebrews 12.1

Tuesday Morning

1   We will proclaim the name of the Lord.
    Ascribe greatness to our God.

Deuteronomy 32.3

Glory to God; Father, Son and Holy Spirit:
    as in the beginning, so now, and for ever. Amen.

2   *The Opening Canticle, A Song of God's Mercy*

God who is rich in mercy:
    out of the great love with which he loved us,

Even when we were dead through our trespasses:
    made us alive together with Christ,

And raised us up with him:
    and made us sit with him
    in the heavenly places in Christ Jesus,

That he might show the immeasurable riches of his grace:
    in kindness towards us in Christ Jesus.

Ephesians 2.4–7

3   *The Opening Prayer*

The night has passed and the day lies open before us;
let us pray with one heart and mind.

    Silence may be kept.

As we rejoice in the gift of this new day,
so may the light of your presence, O God,
set our hearts on fire with love for you;
now and for ever. **Amen.**

    A pause for self-examination, the Confession and Absolution (see Note 1) may be used here.

4   *The Psalms as appointed, or* **Psalm 42***:*

1 As a deer longs for the running brooks:
    so longs my soul for you, O God.

2 My soul is thirsty for God, thirsty for the living God:
   when shall I come and see his face?

3 My tears have been my food day and night:
   while they ask me all day long 'Where now is your God?'

4 As I pour out my soul by myself, I remember this:
   how I went to the house of the Mighty One,
      into the temple of God,

5 To the shouts and songs of thanksgiving:
   a multitude keeping high festival.

6 *Why are you so full of heaviness, my soul:*
   and why so unquiet within me?

7 *O put your trust in God:*
   for I will praise him yet, who is my deliverer and my God.

8 My soul is heavy within me:
   therefore I will remember you from the land of Jordan,
      from Mizar among the hills of Hermon.

9 Deep calls to deep in the roar of your waters:
   all your waves and breakers have gone over me.

10 Surely the Lord will grant his loving mercy in the day-time:
   and in the night his song will be with me,
      a prayer to the God of my life.

11 I will say to God, my rock, 'Why have you forgotten me:
   why must I go like a mourner because the enemy
      oppresses me?'

12 Like a sword through my bones,
      my enemies have mocked me:
   while they ask me all day long 'Where now is your God?'

13 *Why are you so full of heaviness, my soul:*
   and why so unquiet within me?

14 *O put your trust in God:*
   for I will praise him yet, who is my deliverer and my God.

5   *A pause is observed, after which there may follow*

Lord, our God, our Creator, Redeemer, and Sanctifier: we ask you to cleanse us from all hypocrisy, to unite us to our fellow men and women by the bonds of peace and love, and to confirm us in holiness; now and for ever. **Amen.**

6   *One or two Readings from the Bible as appointed.*

The readings may be followed silence for reflection, a hymn or

May your word live in us
and bear much fruit to your glory.

7   *The Canticle, A Song of the Blessed*

Blessed are the poor in spirit:
   for theirs is the kingdom of heaven.

Blessed are those who mourn:
   for they shall be comforted.

Blessed are the meek:
   for they shall inherit the earth.

Blessed are those who hunger and thirst for what is right:
   for they shall be satisfied.

Blessed are the merciful:
   for mercy shall be shown to them.

Blessed are the pure in heart:
   for they shall see God.

Blessed are the peacemakers:
   for they shall be called the children of God.

Blessed are those who are persecuted
for righteousness' sake:
   for theirs is the kingdom of heaven.

Matthew 5.3–10

8   *The Apostles' Creed may be said (Sunday morning 8).*

9   *The Prayers*

Lord have mercy.
Christ have mercy.
Lord have mercy.

10   *The Lord's Prayer and the Collect of the Day*

11   *Intercessions and Thanksgivings may be made according to local custom and need.*

12   *The Morning Collect*

Lord and heavenly Father,
you have brought us safely to this new day:
keep us by your mighty power, protect us from sin,
guard us from every kind of danger,
and in all we do this day
direct us in the fulfilling of your purpose,
through Jesus Christ our Lord. **Amen.**

13   The Lord be with you.
And also with you.
Let us praise the Lord.
Thanks be to God.

May the Lord bless us and keep us; the Lord make his face to shine upon us, and be gracious to us; the Lord lift up his countenance upon us, and give us peace. **Amen.**

Numbers 6.24–26

Tuesday Evening

1   O sing to the Lord a new song:
     sing to the Lord all the earth.

   Glory to God; Father, Son and Holy Spirit:
   as in the beginning, so now, and for ever. Amen.

2   *The Opening Canticle, The Song of the Three*

   Blessed are you, the God of our forebears:
     worthy to be praised and exalted for ever.

   Blessed is your holy and glorious name:
     worthy to be praised and exalted for ever.

   Blessed are you, glorious in your holy temple:
     worthy to be praised and exalted for ever.

   Blessed are you who behold the depths:
     worthy to be praised and exalted for ever.

   Blessed are you on the throne of your kingdom:
     worthy to be praised and exalted for ever.

   Blessed are you in the heights of heaven:
     worthy to be praised and exalted for ever.

Song of the Three 29–34

3   *The Opening Prayer*

   The day is now past and the night is at hand.
   Let us pray with one heart and mind.

     Silence may be kept.

   Father of lights, receive the prayer and praise we offer you
   as our evening sacrifice; make us a light for all the world,
   delivered by your goodness from all the works of darkness;
   through Jesus Christ your Son our Lord. **Amen.**

     *A pause for self-examination, the Confession and Absolution (see
     Note 1) may be used here.*

The Psalms as appointed, or **Psalm 19**:

1 The heavens declare the glory of God:
   and the firmament proclaims his handiwork;

2 One day tells it to another:
   and night to night communicates knowledge.

3 There is no speech or language:
   nor are their voices heard;

4 Yet their sound has gone out through all the world:
   and their words to the ends of the earth.

5 There he has pitched a tent for the sun:
   which comes out as a bridegroom from his chamber,
      and rejoices like a strong man to run his course.

6 Its rising is at one end of the heavens,
      and its circuit to their farthest bound:
   and nothing is hidden from its heat.

7 The law of the Lord is perfect, reviving the soul:
   the command of the Lord is true,
      and makes wise the simple.

8 The precepts of the Lord are right, and rejoice the heart:
   the commandment of the Lord is pure,
      and gives light to the eyes.

9 The fear of the Lord is clean, and endures for ever:
   the judgements of the Lord are unchanging,
      and righteous every one.

10 More to be desired are they than gold, even much fine gold:
   sweeter also than honey, than the honey
      that drips from the comb.

11 Moreover, by them is your servant taught:
   and in keeping them there is great reward.

12 Who can know their own unwitting sins?:
   O cleanse me from my secret faults.

13 Keep your servant also from presumptuous sins,
  lest they get the mastery over me:
  so I shall be clean, and innocent of great offence.
14 May the words of my mouth and the meditation
  of my heart be acceptable in your sight:
  O Lord, my strength and my redeemer.

5   *A pause is observed, after which there may follow*

God of grace, we thank you for all your gifts to us: grant us to accept both pain and joy in faith and hope, and never to fail in love to you and to our sisters and brothers; through Jesus Christ your Son our Lord. **Amen.**

6   *One or two Readings from the Bible as appointed.*

     The readings may be followed by silence for reflection, a hymn, or

May your word live in us
  and bear much fruit to your glory.

7   *The Canticle, The Song of Simeon (Nunc dimittis)*

Now, Lord, you let your servant go in peace:
  your word has been fulfilled.

My own eyes have seen the salvation:
  which you have prepared in the sight of every people:

A light to reveal you to the nations:
  and the glory of your people Israel.

Luke 2.29–32

8 *The Prayers*

Lord have mercy.
  Christ have mercy.
Lord have mercy.

9   *The Lord's Prayer and the Collect of the Day*

10   *Intercessions and Thanksgivings may be made according to local custom and need.*

Be present, merciful God, and protect us through the hours of this night: that we, who are wearied by the changes and chances of this fleeting world, may rest on your eternal changelessness; through Jesus Christ our Lord. **Amen.**

12   The Lord be with you.
      And also with you.
      Let us praise the Lord.
      Thanks be to God.

May Jesus, the Lord of peace, give us peace at all times and in all ways. **Amen.**

2 Thessalonians 3.16

Wednesday Morning

1   Rejoice always; pray without ceasing;
in everything give thanks;
    for this is the will of God in Christ Jesus.

1 Thessalonians 5.16–18

    Glory to God; Father, Son and Holy Spirit:
    as in the beginning, so now, and for ever. Amen.

2   *The Opening Canticle, A Song of God's Grace*

Blessed are you, the God and Father of our Lord Jesus Christ:
    for you have blessed us in Christ Jesus
    with every spiritual blessing in the heavenly places.

You chose us to be yours in Christ
    before the foundation of the world:
    that we should be holy and blameless before you.

In love you destined us to be your children,
    through Jesus Christ:
    according to the purpose of your will,

To the praise of your glorious grace:
    which you freely bestowed on us in the Beloved.

Ephesians 1.3–6

3   *The Opening Prayer*

The night has passed and the day lies open before us;
let us pray with one heart and mind.

    Silence may be kept.

As we rejoice in the gift of this new day,
so may the light of your presence, O God,
set our hearts on fire with love for you;
now and for ever. **Amen.**

    A pause for self-examination, the Confession and Absolution (see Note 1) may be used here.

The Psalms as appointed, or **Psalm 57:**

1 Be merciful to me, O God, be merciful:
    for I come to you for shelter;

2 And in the shadow of your wings will I take refuge:
    until these troubles are over-past.

3 I will call to God Most High:
    to the God who will fulfil his purpose for me.

4 He will send from heaven and save me:
    he will send forth his faithfulness and his loving-kindness,
        and rebuke those that would trample me down.

5 For I lie amidst ravening lions:
    those whose teeth are spears and arrows,
        and their tongue a sharpened sword.

6 *Be exalted, O God, above the heavens:*
    and let your glory be over all the earth.

7 They have set a net for my feet, and I am brought low:
    they have dug a pit before me,
        but shall fall into it themselves.

8 My heart is fixed, O God, my heart is fixed:
    I will sing and make melody.

9 Awake my soul, awake lute and harp:
    for I will awaken the morning.

10 I will give you thanks, O Lord, among the peoples:
    I will sing your praise among the nations.

11 For the greatness of your mercy reaches to the heavens:
    and your faithfulness to the clouds.

12 *Be exalted, O God, above the heavens:*
    and let your glory be over all the earth.

5 *A pause is observed, after which there may follow*

We consecrate this day to your service, O Lord; may all our thoughts, words, and actions be well-pleasing to you and serve the good of our brothers and sisters; through Jesus Christ, our Lord. **Amen.**

6 *One or two Readings from the Bible as appointed.*

The readings may be followed by silence for reflection, a hymn or

May your word live in us
  and bear much fruit to your glory.

7 *The Canticle, Te Deum Laudamus*

We praise you, O God:
  we acclaim you as Lord;

All creation worships you:
  the Father everlasting.

To you all angels, all the powers of heaven:
  the cherubim and seraphim, sing in endless praise:

Holy, holy, holy Lord, God of power and might:
  heaven and earth are full of your glory.

The glorious company of apostles praise you:
  The noble fellowship of prophets praise you.

The white-robed army of martyrs praise you:
  Throughout the world, the holy Church acclaims you:

Father, of majesty unbounded:
  your true and only Son, worthy of all praise,
  the Holy Spirit, advocate and guide.

You, Christ, are the King of glory:
  the eternal Son of the Father.

When you took our flesh to set us free:
  you humbly chose the virgin's womb.

You overcame the sting of death:
and opened the kingdom of heaven to all believers.

You are seated at God's right hand in glory:
We believe that you will come to be our judge.

Come then, Lord, and help your people,
bought with the price of your own blood:
and bring us with your saints to glory everlasting.

8   *The Apostles' Creed may be said (Sunday morning 8).*

9   *The Prayers*

Lord have mercy.
Christ have mercy.
Lord have mercy.

10   *The Lord's Prayer and the Collect of the Day*

11   *Intercessions and Thanksgivings may be made according to local custom and need.*

12   *The Morning Collect*

Eternal God and Father, by whose power we are created and by whose love we are redeemed: guide and strengthen us by your Spirit, that we may give ourselves to your service, and live this day in love to one another and to you; through Jesus Christ our Lord. **Amen.**

13   The Lord be with you.
And also with you.
Let us praise the Lord.
Thanks be to God.

May the God of steadfastness and encouragement grant us to live in such harmony with one another in accord with Christ Jesus, that we may with one voice glorify our God and Father. **Amen.**

Romans 15.5–6

Wednesday Evening

1   Seek the Lord while he may be found;
       call upon him while he is near.

Isaiah 55.6

       Glory to God; Father, Son and Holy Spirit:
       as in the beginning, so now, and for ever. Amen.

2   *The Opening Canticle, A Song of Praise*

God be gracious to us and bless us:
    and make your face to shine upon us,

That your way may be known upon earth:
    your salvation among all nations.

Let the peoples praise you, O God:
    let all the peoples praise you.

Let the nations be glad and sing for joy:
    for you judge the peoples with equity
    and govern the nations upon earth.

Let the peoples praise you, O God:
    let all the peoples praise you.

Then the earth will bring forth its increase:
    and God, our own God, will bless us.

You, O God, will bless us:
    and all the ends of the earth will fear you.

Psalm 67

3   *The Opening Prayer*

The day is now past and the night is at hand.
Let us pray with one heart and mind.

    Silence may be kept.

Father of lights, receive the prayer and praise we offer you
as our evening sacrifice; make us a light for all the world,
delivered by your goodness from all the works of darkness;
through Jesus Christ your Son our Lord. **Amen.**

A pause for self-examination, the Confession and Absolution (see Note 1) may be used here.

4   *The Psalms as appointed, or* **Psalm 46**:

1 God is our refuge and strength:
    a very present help in trouble.

2 Therefore we will not fear, though the earth be moved:
    and though the mountains are shaken
        in the midst of the sea;

3 Though the waters rage and foam:
    and though the mountains quake at the rising of the sea.

4 There is a river whose streams make glad the city of God:
    the holy dwelling-place of the Most High.

5 God is in the midst of her,
        therefore she shall not be moved:
    God will help her, and at break of day.

6 The nations make uproar, and the kingdoms are shaken:
    but God has lifted his voice, and the earth shall tremble.

7 The Lord of hosts is with us:
    the God of Jacob is our stronghold.

8 Come then and see what the Lord has done:
    what destruction he has brought upon the earth.

9 He makes wars to cease in all the world:
    he breaks the bow and shatters the spear,
        and burns the chariots in the fire.

10 'Be still, and know that I am God:
    I will be exalted among the nations,
        I will be exalted upon the earth.'

11 The Lord of hosts is with us:
    the God of Jacob is our stronghold.

5   *A pause is observed, after which there may follow*

God of all power and might, the author and giver of all good things: graft in our hearts the love of your name, increase in us true religion, nourish in us all goodness and, of your great mercy, keep us in the same; through Jesus Christ our Lord. **Amen.**

6   *One or two Readings from the Bible as appointed.*

The readings may be followed by silence for reflection, a hymn, or

May your word live in us
   and bear much fruit to your glory.

7   *The Canticle, The Song of Mary (Magnificat)*

My soul proclaims the greatness of the Lord:
   my spirit rejoices in God my Saviour,

Who has looked with favour on his lowly servant:
   from this day all generations will call me blessed;

The Almighty has done great things for me:
   and holy is his name.

God has mercy on those who fear him:
   from generation to generation.

The Lord has shown strength with his arm:
   and scattered the proud in their conceit,

Casting down the mighty from their thrones:
   and lifting up the lowly.

God has filled the hungry with good things:
   and sent the rich away empty.

He has come to the aid of his servant Israel:
   to remember the promise of mercy,

The promise made to our forebears:
   to Abraham and his children for ever.

Luke 1.46–55

8   *The Prayers*

Lord have mercy.
Christ have mercy.
Lord have mercy.

9   *The Lord's Prayer and the Collect of the Day*

10   *Intercessions and Thanksgivings may be made according to local custom and need.*

11   *The Evening Collect*

Lighten our darkness, Lord, we pray: and in your great mercy defend us from all perils and dangers of this night; for the love of your only Son our Saviour Jesus Christ. **Amen.**

12   The Lord be with you.
And also with you.
Let us praise the Lord.
Thanks be to God.

May our Lord Jesus Christ, and God our Father, comfort our hearts and establish them in every good work and word. **Amen.**

2 Thessalonians 2.16–17

Thursday Morning

1 This is the message we have heard from Christ:
   that God is light, in whom there is no darkness at all.

1 John 1.5

Glory to God; Father, Son and Holy Spirit:
as in the beginning, so now, and for ever. Amen.

2 *The Opening Canticle, A Song of God's Herald*

Go up to a high mountain, herald of good tidings to Zion:
   lift up your voice with strength,
   herald of good tidings to Jerusalem.

Lift up your voice, fear not:
   say to the cities of Judah, 'Behold your God!'

See the Lord God, coming with power:
   coming to rule with his mighty arm.

He brings his reward for the people of God:
   the recompense for those who are saved.

God will feed his flock like a shepherd:
   and gather the lambs in his arms;

He will hold them to his breast:
   and gently lead those that are with young.

Isaiah 40.9–11

3 *The Opening Prayer*

The night has passed and the day lies open before us;
let us pray with one heart and mind.

   Silence may be kept.

As we rejoice in the gift of this new day,
so may the light of your presence, O God,
set our hearts on fire with love for you;
now and for ever. **Amen.**

   *A pause for self-examination, the Confession and Absolution (see
   Note 1) may be used here.*

4 *The Psalms as appointed, or* **Psalm 48**:

1 Great is the Lord and greatly to be praised:
 in the city of our God.

2 High and beautiful is his holy hill:
 it is the joy of all the earth.

3 On Mount Zion, where godhead truly dwells,
  stands the city of the Great King:
 God is well known in her palaces as a sure defence.

4 For the kings of the earth assembled:
 they gathered together and came on;

5 They saw, they were struck dumb:
 they were astonished and fled in terror.

6 Trembling took hold on them, and anguish:
 as on a woman in her travail;

7 Like the breath of the east wind:
 that shatters the ships of Tarshish.

8 As we have heard, so have we seen in the city
  of the Lord of hosts:
 in the city of our God which God has established for ever.

9 We have called to mind your loving-kindness, O God:
 in the midst of your temple.

10 As your name is great, O God, so also is your praise:
 even to the ends of the earth.

11 Your right hand is full of victory let Zion's hill rejoice:
 let the daughters of Judah be glad,
  because of your judgements.

12 Walk about Zion, go round about her,
  and count all her towers:
 consider well her ramparts, pass through her palaces;

13 That you may tell those who come after that such is God:
 our God for ever and ever,
  and he will guide us eternally.

5   *A pause is observed, after which there may follow*

Almighty God, who wonderfully created us in your own image and yet more wonderfully restored us in your Son Jesus Christ: grant that, as he came to share our human nature, so we may be partakers in his divine glory; who is alive and reigns with you and the Holy Spirit, one God, now and for ever. **Amen.**

6   *One or two Readings from the Bible as appointed.*

       The readings may be followed by silence for reflection, a hymn or

May your word live in us
and bear much fruit to your glory.

7   *The Canticle, The Hymn to the Word*

In the beginning was the Word:
  and the Word was with God,

And the Word was God:
  He was in the beginning with God.

All things were made through him:
  and without him, was not anything made that was made.

In him was life:
  and the life was the light of all people.

The light shines in the darkness:
  and the darkness has not overcome it.

He was in the world:
  and the world was made through him
  yet the world knew him not.

He came to his own home:
  and his own people received him not.

But to all who received him who believed on his name:
  he has given power to become children of God;

Who were born not of blood nor of the will of the flesh:
  nor of the will of a man but of God.

And the Word became flesh:
and dwelt among us full of grace and truth;
We have beheld his glory:
glory as of the only Son from the Father.
And from his fullness have we all received:
and grace upon grace.

John 1.1–5, 10–14, 16

8   *The Apostles' Creed may be said (Sunday morning 8).*

9   *The Prayers*

Lord have mercy.
Christ have mercy.
Lord have mercy.

10   *The Lord's Prayer and the Collect of the Day*

11   *Intercessions and Thanksgivings may be made according to local custom and need.*

12   *The Morning Collect*

Lord and heavenly Father,
you have brought us safely to this new day:
keep us by your mighty power, protect us from sin,
guard us from every kind of danger,
and in all we do this day
direct us in the fulfilling of your purpose,
through Jesus Christ our Lord. **Amen.**

13   The Lord be with you.
And also with you.
Let us praise the Lord.
Thanks be to God.

May the God of peace equip us with everything good so that we may do his will; and may he work in us that which is pleasing in his sight; through Jesus Christ, to whom be glory for ever. **Amen.**

see Hebrews 13.20–21

Thursday Evening

1   The Lord our God the Almighty reigns.
    Let us rejoice and exult and give God the glory.

Revelation 19.6–7

Glory to God; Father, Son and Holy Spirit:
    as in the beginning, so now, and for ever. Amen.

2   *The Opening Canticle, A Song of Joy*
Be joyful in the Lord, all the earth:
    serve the Lord with gladness
        and come before his presence with singing.
Know that the Lord is God:
    it is he who has made us, and we are his;
        for we are his people, and the sheep of his pasture.
Enter his gates with thanksgiving;
        go into his courts with praise:
    give thanks to him and praise his name.
For the Lord is good; his loving-kindness is everlasting:
    and his faithfulness endures from age to age.

Psalm 100

3   *The Opening Prayer*
The day is now past and the night is at hand.
Let us pray with one heart and mind.

Silence may be kept.

Father of lights, receive the prayer and praise we offer you as our evening sacrifice; make us a light for all the world, delivered by your goodness from all the works of darkness; through Jesus Christ your Son our Lord. **Amen.**

A pause for self-examination, the Confession and Absolution (see Note 1) may be used here.

4   *The Psalms as appointed, or* **Psalm 47**:

1 O clap your hands, all you peoples:
    and cry aloud to God with shouts of joy.

2 For the Lord Most High is to be feared:
    he is a great king over all the earth.
3 He cast down peoples under us:
    and the nations beneath our feet.
4 He chose us a land for our possession:
    that was the pride of Jacob, whom he loved.
5 God has gone up with the sound of rejoicing:
    and the Lord to the blast of the horn.
6 O sing praises, sing praises to God:
    O sing praises, sing praises to our king.
7 For God is the king of all the earth:
    O praise him in a well-wrought psalm.
8 God has become the king of the nations:
    he has taken his seat upon his holy throne.
9 The princes of the peoples are gathered together:
    with the people of the God of Abraham.
10 For the mighty ones of the earth are become
        the servants of God: and he is greatly exalted.

5   *A pause is observed, after which there may follow*

God our Saviour, you sent Jesus into the world of sin, and
delivered him up to death for us: kindle in our hearts the
same love with which he loved his own to the end; who
lives and reigns with you and the Holy Spirit, one God,
now and for ever. **Amen.**

6   *One or two Readings from the Bible as appointed.*

    The readings may be followed by silence for reflection, a hymn, or

May your word live in us
    and bear much fruit to your glory.

7   *The Canticle, The Song of Christ's Glory*

Christ Jesus was in the form of God:
    but he did not cling to equality with God.

He emptied himself, taking the form of a servant:
and was born in our human likeness.

Being found in human form, he humbled himself:
and became obedient unto death, even death on a cross.

Therefore God has highly exalted him:
and bestowed on him the name above every name,

That at the name of Jesus every knee should bow:
in heaven and on earth and under the earth;

And every tongue confess that Jesus Christ is Lord:
to the glory of God the Father.

Philippians 2.5b–11

8   *The Prayers*

Lord have mercy.
Christ have mercy.
Lord have mercy.

9   *The Lord's Prayer and the Collect of the Day*

10   *Intercessions and Thanksgivings may be made according to local custom and need.*

11   *The Evening Collect*

Be present, merciful God, and protect us through the hours of this night: that we, who are wearied by the changes and chances of this fleeting world, may rest on your eternal changelessness; through Jesus Christ our Lord. **Amen.**

12   The Lord be with you.
And also with you.
Let us praise the Lord.
Thanks be to God.

The grace of the Lord Jesus Christ, and the love of God, and the fellowship of the Holy Spirit, be with us all evermore. **Amen.**

2 Corinthians 13.14

Friday Morning

1   Through Christ let us offer up a sacrifice of praise to God,
the fruit of lips that acknowledge his name.

Hebrews 13.15

Glory to God; Father, Son and Holy Spirit:
as in the beginning, so now, and for ever. Amen.

2   *The Opening Canticle, A Song of God's Grace*

We have complete freedom:
to go into the most holy place by means of the death of Jesus.

He opened for us a new way a living way:
through the curtain, through his own body.

Since we have a great high priest
set over the household of God:
let us draw near with a sincere heart and a sure faith,

With hearts that have been made clean
from a guilty conscience:
and bodies washed with pure water.

Hebrews 10.19–22

3   *The Opening Prayer*

The night has passed and the day lies open before us;
let us pray with one heart and mind.

Silence may be kept.

As we rejoice in the gift of this new day,
so may the light of your presence, O God,
set our hearts on fire with love for you;
now and for ever. **Amen.**

A pause for self-examination, the Confession and Absolution (see Note 1) may be used here.

4   *The Psalms as appointed, or* **Psalm 130**.

1 Out of the depths have I called to you, O Lord:
Lord, hear my voice;

2 O let your ears consider well:
　　the voice of my supplication.

3 If you, Lord, should note what we do wrong:
　　who then, O Lord, could stand?

4 But there is forgiveness with you:
　　so that you shall be feared.

5 I wait for the Lord, my soul waits for him:
　　and in his word is my hope.

6 My soul looks for the Lord:
　　more than watchmen for the morning,
　　　　more, I say, than watchmen for the morning.

7 O Israel, trust in the Lord, for with the Lord there is mercy:
　　and with him is ample redemption.

8 He will redeem Israel:
　　from the multitude of their sins.

5　　*A pause is observed, after which there may follow*

Holy God, through your beloved Son you reconciled all things to yourself, making peace by the blood of his cross: fill us and those for whom we pray with your peace and joy; through Jesus Christ our Lord. **Amen.**

6　　*One or two Readings from the Bible as appointed.*

　　The readings may be followed by silence for reflection, a hymn or

May your word live in us
and bear much fruit to your glory.

7　　*The Canticle, Saviour of the World*

Jesus, Saviour of the world, come to us in your mercy:
　　we look to you to save and help us.

By your cross and your life laid down,
　　you set your people free:
　　we look to you to save and help us.

When they were ready to perish, you saved your disciples:
we look to you to come to our help.

In the greatness of your mercy, loose us from our chains:
forgive the sins of all your people.

Make yourself known as our saviour and mighty deliverer:
save and help us that we may praise you.

Come now and dwell with us, Lord Christ Jesus:
hear our prayer and be with us always.

And when you come in your glory:
make us to be one with you
and to share the life of your kingdom.

8   *The Apostles' Creed may be said (Sunday morning 8).*

9   *The Prayers*

Lord have mercy.
Christ have mercy.
Lord have mercy.

10   *The Lord's Prayer and the Collect of the Day*

11   *Intercessions and Thanksgivings may be made according to local custom and need.*

12   *The Morning Collect*

Eternal God and Father, by whose power we are created and by whose love we are redeemed; guide and strengthen us by your Spirit, that we may give ourselves to your service, and live this day in love to one another and to you; through Jesus Christ our Lord. **Amen.**

13   The Lord be with you.
And also with you.
Let us praise the Lord.
Thanks be to God.

Peace be to us all, and love with faith, from God the Father and the Lord Jesus Christ. **Amen.**   Ephesians 6.23

Friday Evening

1 Peace to those who are far off.
Peace to those who are near.

Ephesians 2.17

Glory to God; Father, Son and Holy Spirit:
as in the beginning, so now, and for ever. Amen.

2 *The Opening Canticle, The Lord's Servant*

He was despised; he was rejected:
  a man of sorrows, acquainted with grief.

As one from whom people hide their faces:
  he was despised, and we esteemed him not.

Ours were the sufferings he bore:
  ours the torments he endured,

While we thought he was being punished:
  struck by God and brought low.

He was pierced for our sins:
  bruised for no fault but ours.

His punishment has won our peace:
  and by his wounds we are healed.

We had all strayed like sheep: all taking our own way;

But the Lord laid on him: the guilt of us all.

Isaiah 53.3–6

3 *The Opening Prayer*

The day is now past and the night is at hand.
Let us pray with one heart and mind.

  Silence may be kept.

Father of lights, receive the prayer and praise we offer you
as our evening sacrifice; make us a light for all the world,
delivered by your goodness from all the works of darkness;
through Jesus Christ your Son our Lord. **Amen.**

A pause for self-examination, the Confession and Absolution (see Note 1) may be used here.

4   *The Psalms as appointed, or* **Psalm 27***:*

1 The Lord is my light and my salvation;
    whom then shall I fear?:
    the Lord is the stronghold of my life;
    of whom shall I be afraid?

2 When the wicked, even my enemies and my foes,
    come upon me to devour me:
    they shall stumble and fall.

3 If an army encamp against me, my heart shall not be afraid:
    and if war should rise against me, yet will I trust.

4 One thing I have asked from the Lord,
    which I will require:
    that I may dwell in the house of the Lord
    all the days of my life,

5 To see the fair beauty of the Lord:
    and to seek his will in his temple.

6 For he will hide me under his shelter in the day of trouble:
    and conceal me in the shadow of his tent,
    and set me high upon a rock.

7 And now he will lift up my head:
    above my enemies round about me.

8 And I will offer sacrifices in his sanctuary with exultation:
    I will sing, I will sing praises to the Lord.

9 O Lord, hear my voice when I cry:
    have mercy upon me and answer me.

10 My heart has said of you, 'Seek his face':
    your face, Lord, I will seek.

11 Do not hide your face from me:
    or thrust your servant aside in displeasure;

12 For you have been my helper:
>   do not cast me away or forsake me,
>   O God of my salvation.

13 Though my father and my mother forsake me:
>   the Lord will take me up.

14 Teach me your way, O Lord:
>   and lead me in an even path, for they lie in wait for me.

15 Do not give me over to the will of my enemies:
>   for false witnesses have risen against me,
>   and those who breathe out violence.

16 But I believe that I shall surely see the goodness
>   of the Lord:
>   in the land of the living.

17 O wait for the Lord;
>   stand firm and he will strengthen your heart:
>   and wait, I say, for the Lord.

5   *A pause is observed, after which there may follow*

Holy Spirit, sanctifier, cleanse us from all hypocrisy, unite us to one another in the bonds of peace and love, and confirm us in holiness, through Jesus Christ our Lord. **Amen.**

6   *One or two Readings from the Bible as appointed.*

   The readings may be followed by silence for reflection, a hymn, or

May your word live in us
and bear much fruit to your glory.

7   *The Canticle, A Song to the Lamb*

You are worthy, our Lord and God:
>   to receive glory and honour and power.

For you have created all things:
>   and by your will they have their being.

You are worthy, O Lamb, for you were slain:
and by your blood you ransomed for God
saints from every tribe and language and nation.
You have made them to be a kingdom and priests
serving our God:
and they will reign with you on earth.
To the One who sits on the throne and to the Lamb
be blessing and honour and glory and might, for ever and
ever. Amen.

Revelation 4.11; 5.9b–10

8   *The Prayers*

Lord have mercy.
Christ have mercy.
Lord have mercy.

9   *The Lord's Prayer and the Collect of the Day*

10   *Intercessions and Thanksgivings may be made according to local custom and need.*

11   *The Evening Collect*

Lighten our darkness, Lord, we pray: and in your great mercy defend us from all perils and dangers of this night; for the love of your only Son our Saviour Jesus Christ. **Amen.**

12   The Lord be with you.
And also with you.
Let us praise the Lord.
Thanks be to God.

May the God of all grace, who has called us to eternal glory in Christ, restore, establish, strengthen us. To him be the dominion for ever and ever. **Amen.**

1 Peter 5.10–11

Saturday Morning

1   God has shone in our hearts,
      **to give the light of the knowledge of the glory of God
      in the face of Jesus Christ.**

2 Corinthians 4.6

      Glory to God; Father, Son and Holy Spirit:
      as in the beginning, so now, and for ever. Amen.

2   *The Opening Canticle, Song of Creation*

      Bless the Lord all created things:
       who is worthy to be praised and exalted for ever.

      Bless the Lord all people of the earth:
       who is worthy to be praised and exalted for ever.

      O people of God bless the Lord:
       bless the Lord you priests of the Lord,

      Bless the Lord you servants of the Lord:
       who is worthy to be praised and exalted for ever.

      Bless the Lord all you of upright spirit:
       bless the Lord you that are holy and humble in heart.

      Bless the Father, the Son and the Holy Spirit:
       who is worthy to be praised and exalted for ever.

Song of the Three 35ff

3   *The Opening Prayer*

      The night has passed and the day lies open before us;
      let us pray with one heart and mind.

       Silence may be kept.

      As we rejoice in the gift of this new day,
      so may the light of your presence, O God,
      set our hearts on fire with love for you;
      now and for ever. **Amen.**

       *A pause for self-examination, the Confession and Absolution (see
       Note 1) may be used here.*

4   *The Psalms as appointed, or* **Psalm 121***;*

1 I lift up my eyes to the hills:
   but where shall I find help?

2 My help comes from the Lord:
   who has made heaven and earth.

3 He will not suffer your foot to stumble:
   and he who watches over you will not sleep.

4 Be sure he who has charge of Israel:
   will neither slumber nor sleep.

5 The Lord himself is your keeper:
   the Lord is your defence upon your right hand;

6 The sun shall not strike you by day:
   nor shall the moon by night.

7 The Lord will defend you from all evil:
   it is he who will guard your life.

8 The Lord will defend your going out and your coming in:
   from this time forward for evermore.

5   *A pause is observed, after which there may follow*

Creator God, whose praise and power are proclaimed by the whole creation: receive our morning prayers, we pray, and renew us in your service; through Jesus Christ our Lord. **Amen.**

6   *One or two Readings from the Bible as appointed.*

        The readings may be followed by silence for reflection, a hymn or

May your word live in us
and bear much fruit to your glory.

7   *The Canticle, A Song of Redemption*

Christ is the image of the invisible God:
   the first-born of all creation.

For in him all things were created:
   in heaven and on earth, visible and invisible.

All things were created through him and for him:
he is before all things and in him all things hold together.

He is the head of the body, the Church:
he is the beginning, the first-born from the dead.

For it pleased God that in him all fullness should dwell:
and through him all things be reconciled to himself.

Colossians 1.15–20

8   *The Apostles' Creed may be said.*

9   *The Prayers*

Lord have mercy.
Christ have mercy.
Lord have mercy.

10   *The Lord's Prayer and the Collect of the Day*

11   *Intercessions and Thanksgivings may be made according to local custom and need.*

12   *The Morning Collect*

Lord and heavenly Father, you have brought us safely to this new day: keep us by your mighty power, protect us from sin, guard us from every kind of danger, and in all we do this day direct us in the fulfilling of your purpose, through Jesus Christ our Lord. **Amen.**

13   The Lord be with you.
And also with you.
Let us praise the Lord.
Thanks be to God.

May the peace of God which passes all understanding keep our hearts and minds in Christ Jesus. **Amen.**

Philippians 4.7

Saturday Evening

1   Grace to you and peace
    from God our Father and the Lord Jesus Christ.
Ephesians 1.2

    Glory to God; Father, Son and Holy Spirit:
    as in the beginning, so now, and for ever. Amen.

2   *The Opening Canticle, Song of the Shepherd*
    The Lord is my shepherd:
        therefore can I lack nothing.

    He shall make me lie down in green pastures:
        and lead me beside still waters.

    He shall refresh my soul:
        and guide me in right pathways for his name's sake.

    Though I walk through the valley of the shadow of death,
    I will fear no evil:
        for you are with me; your rod and your staff comfort me.

    You spread a table before me
    in the presence of those who trouble me:
        you have anointed my head with oil,
        and my cup shall be full.

    Surely your goodness and loving-kindness
    shall follow me all the days of my life:
        and I will dwell in the house of the Lord for ever.

Psalm 23

3   *The Opening Prayer*
    The day is now past and the night is at hand.
    Let us pray with one heart and mind.

        Silence may be kept.
    Father of lights, receive the prayer and praise we offer you
    as our evening sacrifice; make us a light for all the world,
    delivered by your goodness from all the works of darkness;
    through Jesus Christ your Son our Lord. **Amen.**

4   *The Psalms as appointed, or* **Psalm 114***:*

1 When Israel came out of Egypt:
      and the house of Jacob from among a people
            of an alien tongue,

2 Judah became his sanctuary:
      and Israel his dominion.

3 The sea saw that, and fled:
      Jordan was driven back.

4 The mountains skipped like rams:
      and the little hills like young sheep.

5 What ailed you, O sea, that you fled:
      O Jordan, that you were driven back?

6 You mountains, that you skipped like rams:
      and you little hills like young sheep?

7 Tremble, O earth, at the presence of the Lord:
      at the presence of the God of Jacob,

8 Who turned the rock into a pool of water:
      and the flint-stone into a welling spring.

5   *A pause is observed, after which there may follow*

Lord Christ, eternal Word and Light of the Father's glory:
send your light and your truth that we may both know and
proclaim your word of life, to the glory of God the Father;
for you now live and reign, God for all eternity. **Amen.**

6   *One or two Readings from the Bible as appointed. The readings*
      may be followed by silence for reflection, a hymn or

May your word live in us
      and bear much fruit to your glory.

7   *The Canticle, the Easter Anthems*

Christ our Passover has been sacrificed for us:
      so let us celebrate the feast,

Not with the old leaven of corruption and wickedness:
      but with the unleavened bread of sincerity and truth.

Christ once raised from the dead dies no more:
death has no more dominion over him.

In dying, he died to sin once for all:
in living, he lives to God.

See yourselves, therefore, as dead to sin:
and alive to God in Jesus Christ our Lord.

Christ has been raised from the dead:
the first fruits of those who sleep.

For since by one man came death:
by another has come also the resurrection of the dead,

For as in Adam all die:
even so in Christ shall all be made alive.

8   *The Prayers*

Lord have mercy.
Christ have mercy.
Lord have mercy.

9   *The Lord's Prayer and the Collect of the Day*

10   *Intercessions and Thanksgivings may be made according to local custom and need.*

11   *The Evening Collect*

Come to visit us, Lord, this night, so that by your strength we may rise at daybreak to rejoice in the resurrection of Christ your Son, who lives and reigns for ever and ever. **Amen.**

12   The Lord be with you.
And also with you.
Let us praise the Lord.
Thanks be to God.

I am the Alpha and the Omega, says the Lord, the first and the last, the beginning and the end. **Amen.**

see Revelation 22.13, 20

Additional Canticles

1   *The Song of Zechariah (Benedictus)*

Blessed are you, Lord, the God of Israel:
    you have come to your people and set them free.

You have raised up for us a mighty Saviour:
    born of the house of your servant David.

Through your holy prophets, you promised of old:
    to save us from our enemies, from the hands of
    all who hate us,

To show mercy to our forebears:
    and to remember your holy covenant.

This was the oath God swore to our father Abraham:
    to set us free from the hands of our enemies,

Free to worship you without fear:
    holy and righteous before you, all the days of our life.

And you, child, shall be called the prophet of the Most High:
    for you will go before the Lord to prepare the way,

To give God's people knowledge of salvation:
    by the forgiveness of their sins.

In the tender compassion of our God:
    the dawn from on high shall break upon us,

To shine on those who dwell in darkness
and the shadow of death:
    and to guide our feet into the way of peace.

Luke 1.68–79

2   *The Song of Mary (Magnificat)*

My soul proclaims the greatness of the Lord:
    my spirit rejoices in God my Saviour,

For you, Lord, have looked with favour on your lowly servant:
    From this day all generations will call me blessed.

You, the Almighty, have done great things for me:
    and holy is your name.

You have mercy on those who fear you:
   from generation to generation.

You have shown strength with your arm:
   and scattered the proud in their conceit,

Casting down the mighty from their thrones:
   and lifting up the lowly.

You have filled the hungry with good things:
   and sent the rich away empty.

You have come to the aid of your servant Israel:
   to remember the promise of mercy,

The promise made to our forebears:
   to Abraham and his children for ever.

Luke 1.46–55

3   *Great and Wonderful*

Great and wonderful are your deeds:
   Lord God the Almighty.

Just and true are your ways:
   O ruler of the nations.

Who shall not revere you and praise your name O Lord?:
   for you alone are holy.

All nations shall come and worship in your presence:
   for your just dealings have been revealed.

To the One who sits on the throne and to the Lamb:
   be praise and honour glory and might
   for ever and ever. Amen.

Revelation 15.3–4

4   *A Song of the Word of the Lord*

Seek the Lord while he may be found:
   call upon him while he is near;

Let the wicked abandon their ways:
   and the unrighteous their thoughts;

Return to the Lord, who will have mercy:
   to our God, who will richly pardon.

'For my thoughts are not your thoughts:
  neither are your ways my ways', says the Lord.

'For as the heavens are higher than the earth:
  so are my ways higher than your ways
  and my thoughts than your thoughts.

'As the rain and the snow come down from above:
  and return not again but water the earth,

'Bringing forth life and giving growth:
  seed for sowing and bread to eat,

'So is my word that goes forth from my mouth:
  it will not return to me fruitless,

'But it will accomplish that which I purpose:
  and succeed in the task I gave it.'

Isaiah 55.6–11

5   *A Song of Creation (Song of the Three 35–65)*

Bless the Lord all created things,
  who is worthy to be praised and exalted for ever.

Bless the Lord you heavens,
  who is worthy to be praised and exalted for ever.

Bless the Lord you angels of the Lord,
  bless the Lord all you his hosts,

bless the Lord you waters above the heavens,
  who is worthy to be praised and exalted for ever.

Bless the Lord sun and moon,
bless the Lord you stars of heaven,
bless the Lord all rain and dew,
  who is worthy to be praised and exalted for ever.

Bless the Lord all winds that blow,
bless the Lord you fire and heat,
bless the Lord scorching wind and bitter cold,
  who is worthy to be praised and exalted for ever.

Bless the Lord dews and falling snows,
bless the Lord you nights and days,

bless the Lord light and darkness,
who is worthy to be praised and exalted for ever.

Bless the Lord frost and cold,
bless the Lord you ice and snow,
bless the Lord lightning and clouds,
who is worthy to be praised and exalted for ever.

O let the earth bless the Lord;
bless the Lord you mountains and hills,
bless the Lord all that grows in the ground,
who is worthy to be praised and exalted for ever.

Bless the Lord you springs,
bless the Lord you seas and rivers,
bless the Lord you whales and all that swim in the waters,
who is worthy to be praised and exalted for ever.

Bless the Lord all birds of the air,
bless the Lord you beasts and cattle,
bless the Lord all people of the earth,
who is worthy to be praised and exalted for ever.

O People of God bless the Lord;
bless the Lord you priests of the Lord,
bless the Lord you servants of the Lord,
who is worthy to be praised and exalted for ever.

Bless the Lord all you of upright spirit,
bless the Lord you that are holy and humble in heart,
bless the Father, the Son and the Holy Spirit,
who is worthy to be praised and exalted for ever.

6   *A Song of the Knowledge of Wisdom*
O God of our ancestors and Lord of mercy:
you have made all things by your word.

By your wisdom you have formed us:
to have dominion over all your creation,

To be stewards of the world in holiness and righteousness:
and to administer justice with an upright heart.

Give us Wisdom who sits by your throne:
  do not refuse us a place among your servants,

For Wisdom knows your works:
  and was present when you made the world.

She understands what is pleasing in your sight:
  and what accords with your commandments.

Send her from the holy heavens:
  from the throne of your glory bid her come,

That she may labour at our side:
  and we may learn what is pleasing to you.

For she knows and understands all things:
  and will guide us prudently in our actions
  and protect us with her glory.

Wisdom 9.1–6, 9–11

7   *A Song of Christ's Goodness*

Jesus, as a mother you gather your people to you:
  you are gentle with us as a mother with her children.

Often you weep over our sins and our pride:
  tenderly you draw us from hatred and judgement.

You comfort us in sorrow and bind up our wounds:
  in sickness you nurse us and with pure milk you feed us.

Jesus, by your dying, we are born to new life:
  by your anguish and labour we come forth in joy.

Despair turns to hope through your sweet goodness:
  through your gentleness, we find comfort in fear.

Your warmth gives life to the dead:
  your touch makes sinners righteous.

Lord Jesus, in your mercy, heal us:
  in your love and tenderness, remake us.

In your compassion, bring grace and forgiveness:
  for the beauty of heaven, may your love prepare us.

Anselm of Canterbury

8   *A Song of Christ the Servant*

Christ suffered for us, leaving us an example:
  that we should follow in his steps.

He committed no sin, no guile was found on his lips:
  when he was reviled, he did not revile in turn.

When he suffered, he did not threaten:
  but he trusted in God who judges justly.

Christ himself bore our sins in his body on the tree:
  that we might die to sin and live to righteousness.

By his wounds, we have been healed
for we were straying like sheep:
  but have now returned
  to the Shepherd and Guardian of our souls.

1 Peter 2.21–25

9   *A Song of True Motherhood*

God chose to be our mother in all things:
  and so made the foundation of his work,
  most humbly and most pure, in the Virgin's womb.

God, the perfect wisdom of all:
  arrayed himself in this humble place.

Christ came in our poor flesh:
  to share a mother's care.

Our mothers bear us for pain and for death:
  our true mother, Jesus, bears us for joy and endless life.

Christ carried us within him in love and travail:
  until the full time of his passion.

And when all was completed and he carried us so for joy:
  still all this could not satisfy the power of his wonderful love.

All that we owe is redeemed in truly loving God:
  for the love of Christ works in us;
  Christ is the one whom we love.

Based on Julian of Norwich

10   *The Song of Hannah*

My heart exults in the Lord:
  my strength is exalted in my God.

My mouth derides my enemies:
  because I rejoice in your salvation.

There is no Holy One like you, O Lord:
  nor any Rock like you, our God.

For you are a God of knowledge:
  and by you our actions are weighed.

The bows of the mighty are broken:
  but the feeble gird on strength.

Those who were full now search for bread:
  but those who were hungry are well fed.

The barren woman has borne sevenfold:
  but she who has many children is forlorn.

Both the poor and the rich are of your making:
  you bring low and you also exalt.

You raise up the poor from the dust:
  and lift the needy from the ash heap.

You make them sit with the rulers:
  and inherit a place of honour.

For the pillars of the earth are yours:
  and on them you have set the world.

1 Samuel 2.1–8

Notes

1   This confession may be used on Sunday morning,
     and in each evening service at ¶3:

Merciful God,
our maker and our judge,
we have sinned against you in thought, word, and deed,
and in what we have failed to do:
we have not loved you with our whole heart;
we have not loved our neighbours as ourselves;
we repent, and are sorry for all our sins.
Father, forgive us.
Strengthen us to love and obey you in newness of life;
through Jesus Christ our Lord. Amen.

The priest says this absolution

Almighty God have mercy on you,
forgive you all your sins through our Lord Jesus Christ,
strengthen you in all goodness,
and by the power of the Holy Spirit
keep you in eternal life. Amen.

Or the minister may say this word of assurance

If we confess our sins, God who is faithful and just will forgive
us our sins and cleanse us from all unrighteousness. (1 John 1:9)

2   If the daily services are used independently of the Holy Communion as
     a public service on Sundays, the Apostles' Creed should be used in the
     morning and the confession used at ¶ 3.

3   The following collects may be used as a psalm prayer at ¶ 5.

During Advent
     Almighty God, give us grace that we may cast away the works of
     darkness and put on the armour of light, now in the time of this mortal
     life in which your Son Jesus Christ came among us in great humility;
     that on the last day, when he comes again in his glorious majesty to
     judge the living and the dead, we may rise to the life immortal; through
     him who lives and reigns with you and the Holy Spirit, now and for
     ever. **Amen.**

During Lent

Almighty and everlasting God, you hate nothing you have made, and you forgive the sins of all who are penitent: create and make in us new and contrite hearts, that we, lamenting our sins and acknowledging our wretchedness, may obtain from you, the God of all mercy, perfect remission and forgiveness; through Jesus Christ our Lord. **Amen.**

During Easter

Almighty God, you have conquered death through your dearly beloved Son Jesus Christ and opened to us the gate of everlasting life: grant us by your grace to set our mind on things above, so that by your continual help our whole life may be transformed; through Jesus Christ our Lord, who is alive and reigns with you and the Holy Spirit in everlasting glory. **Amen.**

4   An Office hymn may be used after the psalm prayer at ¶ 5.

5   The *Gloria Patri* is printed at the beginning of each of the services, but may also be said after the set canticles.

6   **The Canticles**

Those who wish to say a canticle after each reading may use the set canticles after the first reading and the gospel canticles —
the Song of Zechariah (*Benedictus*) and the Song of Mary (*Magnificat*) —
after the second reading.

It will be necessary to select another canticle from the daily services or additional canticles when either of the gospel canticles is set for the day.

The gospel canticles may also be used daily instead of the set canticles at ¶ 7, the *Benedictus* in the morning and the *Magnificat* in the evening. The displaced canticles may be used as one of the psalms for the day.

Additional Canticles 1 and 2 provide alternative ELLC translations of the *Benedictus* and *Magnificat* which address God in the second person.

7   This order expands the pattern of *An Australian Prayer Book in* focusing on a seasonal theme for certain days:

Sunday celebrates the resurrection, and may be used daily in the Easter season.

Monday focuses on the ministry of the Holy Spirit and may be used daily in the week after Pentecost and for Saints' days.

Thursday's office is based around the theme of incarnation and may be used daily through Christmas and Epiphany.

Friday carries the theme of the cross and may be used daily in the season of Lent and Holy Week.

Saturday touches on the theme of creation and may be found a useful beginning to what for many is a day of recreation.

The Additional Canticles may be useful during these or other seasons of the Church's year.

8   Patterns for intercession and thanksgiving are found in *Prayers for Various Occasions*.

9   The Grace may be used at each daily service instead of the Scripture prayer at ¶ 13 in the morning and ¶ 12 in the evening.

10   Selections from these services may be made for family or small group prayers. The following arrangement is one suitable form:

Opening sentence, canticle and prayer,
followed by a shorter psalm portion,
a Bible reading and canticle,
Lord's Prayer and other prayers.

Prayer at the End of the Day

ALSO CALLED COMPLINE

1   *The minister says*

The Lord almighty grant us a quiet night and a perfect end.
Amen.

[2   *A period of silence may be kept for reflection on the past day.*

When the confession has not been used at Evening Prayer, it may be used here. The form provided in Evening Prayer may be used, or the following.

Lord Jesus, you came to call sinners to repentance,
    have mercy on us.
Lord Jesus, sent to heal those who are burdened in soul,
    have mercy on us.
Lord Jesus, now seated at the Father's right hand to intercede for us.
    have mercy on us.]

3   *The minister says*

Our help is in the name of the Lord,
    who made heaven and earth.
    Glory to God; Father, Son and Holy Spirit:
    as in the beginning, so now, and for ever.
    Praise the Lord!

4   *This hymn, or another, may be sung.*

Hail, gladdening Light, of his pure glory poured
Who is the immortal Father, heavenly, blest,
Holiest of Holies, Jesus Christ, our Lord.

Now we come to the sun's hour of rest,
The lights of evening round us shine,
We hymn the Father, Son, and Holy Spirit divine.

Worthiest art thou at all times to be sung
with undefiled tongue,
Son of God, giver of life, alone!
Therefore in all the world they glories, Lord, they own.

5   *One of more of Psalms 4, 91 and 134 is said or sung.*

Psalm 4

1 Answer me when I call, O God of my righteousness:
    you set me free when I was hard-pressed;
  have mercy on me now and hear my prayer.

2 How long, you people, will you turn my honour into shame:
    how long will you love what is worthless
    and seek after falsehood?

3 Know that the Lord has shown me wonderful kindness:
    when I call upon the Lord, the Lord will hear me.

4 Tremble, then, and do not sin:
    commune with your own heart upon your bed and be still.

5 Offer sacrifices that are right:
    and put your trust in the Lord.

6 There are many who say, 'Who can show us any good?:
    The light of your countenance has departed from us,
      O Lord.'

7 Yet you have put more gladness in my heart:
    than they have when grain and new wine abound.

8 I will lie down in peace and sleep:
    for it is only you, O Lord, who make me dwell in safety.

Psalm 91

1 Those who dwell in the shelter of the Most High:
    who abide under the shadow of the Almighty,

2 They shall say to the Lord,
      'You are my refuge and my stronghold:
    my God in whom I put my trust.'

3 'Surely I shall deliver you,' says the Lord,
   'from the snare of the hunter:
   and from the deadly pestilence.

4 I shall cover you with my feathers,
   and you will be safe under my wings:
   my faithfulness will be your shield and defence.

5 You shall not be afraid of any terror by night:
   nor of the arrow that flies by day;

6 Of the pestilence that stalks in the darkness:
   nor of the plague that destroys at noon.

7 A thousand may fall beside you and ten thousand
   at your right hand:
   but you it shall not come near.

8 Your eyes have only to look: to see the reward of the wicked.

9 Because you have made the Lord your refuge:
   and the Most High your stronghold,

10 No evil shall happen to you:
   nor shall any plague come near your dwelling.

11 For I shall give my angels charge over you:
   to keep you in all your ways.

12 They will lift you up in their hands:
   lest you dash your foot against a stone.

13 You will tread upon the lion and the adder:
   you will trample the young lion and serpent under your feet.

14 Because you are bound to me in love,
   therefore I will deliver you:
   I will protect you, because you know my name.

15 You will call upon me, and I shall answer you:
   I will be with you in trouble;
   I will rescue you and bring you to honour.

16 With long life will I satisfy you:
   and show you my salvation.'

Psalm 134

1 Come now, praise the Lord, all you servants of the Lord:
    you that stand by night in the house of the Lord.

2 Lift up your hands in the holy place and praise the Lord:
    May the Lord bless you from Zion,
        the Lord who made heaven and earth.

*The following arrangement of Psalms is also suitable: Sunday 91,
Monday 86, Tuesday 143.1–11, Wednesday 31.1–6 and 130,
Thursday 16, Friday 88, Saturday 4 and 134.*

6   *The following, or some other reading from the Bible*

Sunday   The servants of God shall see his face, and his name
will be on their foreheads. And there will be no more night;
they need no light of lamp or sun, for the Lord God will be
their light, and they shall reign for ever and ever.

Revelation 22.4-5

Monday   I will pour out my spirit on all flesh; your sons and
your daughters shall prophesy, your old men shall dream
dreams, and your young men shall see visions.   Joel 2.28

Tuesday   Discipline yourselves, keep alert. Like a roaring lion
your adversary the devil prowls around, looking for some-
one to devour. Resist him, steadfast in your faith. 1 Peter 5.8-9a

Wednesday   In him was life, and the life was the light of all
people. The light shines in the darkness, and the darkness
has not overcome it.   John 1.4-5

Thursday   Be angry but do not sin; do not let the sun go down
on your anger, and do not make room for the devil.

Ephesians 4.26–27

Friday   For God has destined us not for wrath but for
obtaining salvation through our Lord Jesus Christ, who
died for us, so that whether we are awake or asleep we may
live with him.   1 Thessalonians 5.9-10

Saturday   Hear O Israel: the Lord is our God, the Lord alone. You shall love the Lord your God with all your heart, and with all your soul, and with all your might. Keep these words that I am commanding you today in your heart. Recite them to your children and talk about them when you are at home, and when you are away, when you lie down and when you arise.   Deuteronomy 6.4-7

After the reading the congregation may respond
Thanks be to God.

and/or the following may be said or sung.

Into your hands, Lord, I commend my spirit.
[Alleluia, alleluia.]
Into your hands, Lord, I commend my spirit.
[Alleluia, alleluia.]

You have redeemed us, Lord, God of truth.
I commend my spirit. [Alleluia, alleluia.]

Glory to God; Father, Son, and Holy Spirit.
Into your hands, Lord, I commend my spirit.
[Alleluia, alleluia.]

7   *The Canticle, the Song of Simeon (Luke 2.29ff) is said or sung.*

Save us, Lord, while we are awake;
   protect us while we are asleep;
      that we may keep watch with Christ
      and rest with him in peace.

Now, Lord, you let your servant go in peace:
   your word has been fulfilled.

My own eyes have seen the salvation:
   which you have prepared in the sight of every people:

A light to reveal you to the nations:
   and the glory of your people Israel.

[Save us, Lord, while we are awake;
protect us while we are asleep;
that we may keep watch with Christ
and rest with him in peace.]

8   *The prayers*

Lord have mercy.
    Christ have mercy.
Lord have mercy.

**Our Father in heaven,
    hallowed be your name,
    your kingdom come,
    your will be done,
        on earth as in heaven.
Give us today our daily bread.
Forgive us our sins
    as we forgive those who sin against us.
Save us from the time of trial
    and deliver us from evil.
For the kingdom, the power, and the glory are yours
now and for ever. Amen.**

*Intercessions and thanksgivings may be made according to local
custom.*

9   *The service ends with one or more of the following prayers.*

In your mercy, Lord, dispel the darkness of this night.
Let your household so sleep in peace
that at the dawn of a new day
they may with joy waken in your name;
through Christ our Lord. **Amen.**

Lighten our darkness, Lord, we pray: and in your great
mercy defend us from all perils and dangers of this night;
for the love of your only Son our Saviour Jesus Christ.
Amen.

Lord, be the guest of this *house*;
keep far from it all the deceits of the evil one.
May your holy angels watch over us
as guardians of our peace.
And may your blessing be always upon us,
through Jesus Christ our Lord.
Amen

Lord Jesus Christ, Son of the living God,
who at this evening hour rested in the sepulchre,
and sanctified the grave to be a bed of hope to your people:
make us so to abound in sorrow for our sins,
which were the cause of your passion,
that when our bodies lie in the dust
we may live with you,
through the saving merits of your cross;
for you live and reign with the Father and the Holy Spirit,
one God, now and for ever.
Amen.

As watchmen look for the morning
so we wait eagerly for you, O Lord.
Come with the dawning of the day
and make yourself known to us in the breaking of the bread,
for you are our God for ever and ever.
Amen.

Come, O Spirit of God,
and make within us your dwelling place and home.
May our darkness be dispelled by your light,
and our troubles calmed by your peace;
may all evil be redeemed by your love,
all pain transformed through the suffering of Christ,
and all dying glorified by his risen life.
Amen.

We give you thanks, O God,
for the gift to the world of our Redeemer;
as we sing of your glory at the close of this day,
so may we know his presence in our hearts;
who is our Saviour and our God,
now and for ever.
Amen.

Suitable on Sunday

God our Father,
as we have celebrated today
    the mystery of the Lord's resurrection,
grant our humble prayer;
free us from all harm,
that we may sleep in peace
    and rise in joy to sing your praise;
through Christ our Lord.
Amen.

Suitable on Saturday

Come to visit us, Lord, this night,
so that by your strength we may rise at daybreak
to rejoice in the resurrection of Christ your Son,
who lives and reigns for ever and ever.
Amen.

10   *The minister concludes the service by saying*

Let us praise the Father, the Son and the Holy Spirit;
    God is worthy to be praised and exalted for ever.

May the almighty and merciful God bless us and keep us.
Amen.

Prayers for Various Occasions

Prayers for the World and the Nation

1   Peace

God of the nations, whose sovereign rule brings justice and peace,
have mercy on our broken and divided world.
Shed abroad your peace in the hearts of all
and banish from them the spirit that makes for war,
that all races and peoples may learn to live
as members of one family and in obedience to your law,
through your Son Jesus Christ our Lord. **Amen.**

2   In times of national / international tension

Almighty God, ruler of all,
in whose kingdom peace and righteousness abound;
we pray for those who are in conflict …
Take away prejudice, cruelty and revenge.
Grant that barriers which divide may crumble,
suspicions disappear and hatreds cease,
through Jesus Christ our mediator. **Amen.**

3   In times of conflict

God our refuge and strength,
you have bound us together in a common life:
help us, in the midst of our present conflict
to confront one another without hatred or bitterness
to listen for your voice amid competing claims
and to work together with mutual forbearance and respect;
through Jesus Christ our Lord. **Amen.**

4   Good government

Spirit of justice and truth,
grant to our governments, and all who serve in public life,
wisdom and skill, imagination and energy;
protect them from corruption and the temptation of self-serving.

Help us to commit ourselves to the common good
that our land may be a secure home for all its peoples,
through Jesus Christ the Prince of Peace. **Amen.**

5 Parliament

Most gracious God, ruler of the nations,
we pray for the Parliament of this *State/Territory/Commonwealth*,
   its members and officers [*and especially for…*].
Direct their work and influence their decisions
   to the advancement of your glory,
   and the safety and welfare of this country,
so that peace and happiness, truth and justice,
   may be established among us;
through Jesus Christ our Lord. **Amen.**

6 Australia

God, bless Australia,
guard our people
guide our leaders
and give us peace;
for Jesus Christ's sake. **Amen.**

7 Reconciliation

Lord God, bring us together as one,
   reconciled with you and reconciled with each other.
You made us in your likeness,
   you gave us your Son, Jesus Christ.
He has given us forgiveness from sin.
Lord God, bring us together as one,
   different in culture, but given new life in Jesus Christ,
   together as your body, your Church, your people.
Lord God, bring us together as one,
   reconciled, healed, forgiven,
   sharing you with others as you have called us to do.
In Jesus Christ, let us be together as one. **Amen.**

8   Australia Day

We bless you, God of the universe, for this land,
>   for its contrasts of landscape and climate,
>   for its abundance of wealth and opportunity.
We bless you for our history,
>   with all its struggles in adversity,
>   its courage and hope.
Give us in our diversity tolerance and respect for each other
>   and a passionate commitment to justice for all.
Bless us so that we might be a blessing to others.
We ask this through Jesus Christ our Lord. **Amen.**

9   On Anzac Day

God of love and liberty,
we bring our thanks today for the peace and security we enjoy.
We remember those who in time of war
>   faithfully served their country.
We pray for their families,
>   and for ourselves whose freedom was won at such a cost.
Make us a people zealous for peace,
and hasten the day when nation
>   shall not lift up sword against nation
>   neither learn war any more.
This we pray in the name of the one who gave his life
>   for the sake of the world:
Jesus Christ, our Redeemer. **Amen.**

10   Defence and Police Forces

Eternal God, the only source of peace,
we pray for all who serve in the defence
>   and police forces of this land.
Give them courage and comfort in danger,
>   patience in waiting, and discipline in the just use of force.
Help us to seek for all people the freedom
>   to serve you and each other in compassion and peace.
We ask this through Jesus Christ our Lord. **Amen.**

11 Seafarers

Heavenly Father, we commend to you all seafarers.
Guard and protect them in danger and temptation;
    sustain them in loneliness;
    and support them in sickness and anxiety.
Bless all who minister to them.
Watch over those who are near and dear to them,
    and grant them the blessing of your presence.
These things we ask though Jesus Christ our Lord. Amen.

12 In time of drought, flood or bushfire

All things look to you, O Lord,
to give them their food in due season:
look in mercy on your people,
    and hear our prayer for those whose lives and possessions
    are threatened [*have been destroyed*] by drought [*flood, fire*].
In your mercy restore your creation and heal our land.
So guide and bless your people,
    that we may enjoy the fruits of the earth
    and give you thanks with grateful hearts,
through our Lord Jesus Christ. **Amen.**

13 Rain

God our heavenly Father
through your Son you promised
to those seeking first your kingdom
    and your righteousness
all things necessary for bodily welfare:
send us, we pray, in this time of need,
rain to water the earth,
that we may receive its produce
    to strengthen and sustain us
and always praise your for your bounty;
through Jesus Christ our Lord. **Amen.**

Prayers for Society and the Common Life

14   Places of learning

God of all truth,
teach us to love you with heart and mind.
Bless our schools, colleges and universities [*especially...*]
that they may be lively centres for sound learning,
    new discovery, and the pursuit of wisdom.
May all who teach and all who learn
    seek and love the truth,
and in humility look to you,
the source of all wisdom and understanding,
through Jesus Christ our Lord. **Amen.**

15   Our homes

Almighty God and heavenly Father,
your Son Jesus Christ shared at Nazareth
    the life of an earthly home.
Bless our homes, we pray
that parents and children may be bound to each other
    by mutual love and honour,
and come to a knowledge of your love for them;
through Jesus Christ our Lord. **Amen.**

16   Our homes

Visit Lord, our homes
and drive far from them all the snares of the evil one:
let your holy angels dwell in them to preserve us in peace
and may your blessing rest upon us evermore;
through Jesus Christ our Lord. **Amen.**

17   The media

Almighty God,
you proclaim your truth in every age by many voices:
Direct those who speak where many listen,
    those who write what many read
    those who influence what many see,

that they may do their part
in making the heart of this people wise,
its mind sound
and its will righteous
to the honour of Jesus Christ, our Lord. **Amen.**

18 Judicial system

Great Judge of all,
give understanding and integrity to our judges and magistrates,
so that they may discern the truth,
safeguard human rights, and administer the law with justice.
Enable them to make wise decisions
for the well-being of individuals and society
so that you may be faithfully served and your name honoured;
through Jesus Christ our Lord. **Amen.**

19 Industry and business

God of all creation,
we pray for all who work in the offices and factories of this land.
Enable them to live and work together in harmony and safety,
and offer to you the fruits of their toil for the good of all.
Give respect and dignity to all who labour, discernment and skill
to those who develop new technologies,
and wisdom to all who carry great responsibilities.
You have given us the knowledge to produce plenty;
give us also the will to bring it within the reach of all,
through Jesus Christ our Lord. **Amen.**

20 Those who are absent

God of every place,
we pray for loved ones absent from us:
protect them from harm, direct them in your way
and strengthen them in difficulty.
Give them a firm trust in you and your goodness
through Jesus Christ our Saviour. **Amen.**

21 Good use of leisure

O God, our rest and our redeemer,
in the course of this busy life
give us times of refreshment and peace,
to rebuild our bodies and renew our minds,
so that we may live in harmony with you and your creation;
though Jesus Christ our Lord. **Amen.**

Prayers for those in Need

22 For those experiencing guilt and anxiety

God of all comfort:
quieten our minds
that we may make room for your healing forgiveness;
through Jesus Christ our Lord. **Amen.**

God of love and wisdom,
you know all our anxieties and fears:
grant that N may cast all *her* care on you,
knowing that you care for *her*.
Give *her* quietness of mind,
an unshaken trust in you,
and keep *her* in your perfect peace;
through Jesus Christ our Lord. **Amen.**

23 For one facing an operation

God of compassion and mercy,
you never fail to help and comfort those who seek your aid;
give strength and peace to this your *son/daughter*.
and enable *him* to know that you are near.
Give wisdom and care to those who minister to *him*
especiallyÉ;
grant that *he* may have no fear
since you are with *him*;
through Jesus Christ our Lord. **Amen.**

24   For one recovering from an operation

Almighty God,
source of all life and health:
we give you thanks for human knowledge and medical skills,
for nurses and doctors,
and all those whose hands have brought the gift of healing.
Continue to make N whole in body, mind and spirit;
through Jesus Christ our Lord. **Amen.**

25   For one with a life-threatening illness

God our refuge,
when human resources fail,
you alone remain our sure hope and defence.
In the knowledge of our love, grant us courage.
We place ourselves in your hands,
confident that nothing can separate us from you love,
in Christ Jesus our Lord. **Amen.**

26   The aged

Lord God, the giver of eternal life,
we pray for the elderly of our community
and thank you for those who, having given a lifetime of service,
     face the future with faith.
We remember too, the housebound, the lonely and fearful,
     the doubting and the despairing.
Bless them all, and fill with love those who serve them;
     through Jesus Christ, our Saviour. **Amen**

27   The unemployed

Heavenly Father, we remember before you
those who suffer want and anxiety from lack of employment.
Guide the people of this land to use their wealth and resources
so that everyone may find suitable and fulfilling work.
May all receive just payment and recognition for their labour,
and offer the fruit of their toil in service to you and one another;
through your Son, Jesus Christ our Lord. **Amen.**

28   A prayer in doubt and tested faith

Almighty God our heavenly Father,
what you ask us to bear at times we find hard to understand.
Sometimes we feel angry and confused,
when your care and purpose seem distant,
and we fear that in our faith we have been deceived.
Yet we believe that you are still our heavenly Father,
and we long to know that your love has not lost control.
Strengthen our faith and assure us of your gracious compassion.
Through Jesus Christ our Lord. **Amen.**

29   Prayer for those suffering severe illness

Healing Spirit,
we pray for those suffering from serious diseases
and for those who are terminally ill,
and those living with HIV/AIDS.
We pray for skill and patience for the doctors and nurses who
care for them.
We pray that their relatives and friends
may be strengthened and comforted.
May their faith not falter
as they support each other through testing times.
We pray for those engaged in research
that by your inspiration and their skill
the scourges of this generation may be overcome.
Help us to live in your way
and to seek healing in body, mind and spirit. **Amen**

30   The poor and neglected

God of mercy and pity, remember the homeless, the destitute, the
sick, the aged, and all who have none to care for them.
Heal those who are broken in body or spirit,
    and turn their sorrow into joy.
Help us to minister to their needs, for the love of your Son,
    who for our sake became poor,
    Jesus Christ our Lord. **Amen.**

30 Family breakdown

God of peace,
we pray for families in crisis.
Heal the broken-hearted, and bind up the wounded;
 comfort and sustain them in their need.
Give them wise and faithful friends,
grace to forgive and be forgiven,
and courage for the road ahead,
in the name of Jesus. **Amen.**

31 Those suffering abuse

Loving God,
whose Son was both victim and victor,
we cry to you for those who suffer abuse,
[*especially…*].

Be with *them* in confusion and pain.
Heal the wounds of body and mind;
break open the prisons of fear, self-doubt and despair;
and strengthen *them* to face the future
 with faith, hope and courage.
Reach out to *them* with your love,
 that they may be made whole in body, mind and spirit,
 through the healing touch of the suffering Christ. **Amen**

32 Those suffering abuse

God, our redeemer and sustainer,
we pray for survivors of violence, abuse and neglect.
Give your power to the powerless,
 your fullness to the empty of spirit.
Heal their wounds, free them from fear,
 and restore them to true health.
Grant this through Jesus Christ,
 the crucified and risen Saviour
who is alive and reigns with you and the Holy Spirit,
one God, for ever and ever. **Amen.**

33   Those who abuse

Judge of all the earth,
God of justice,
we bring before you all who abuse others.
Turn the hearts of the violent from the way of evil.
Fill them with a hatred of the damage they do,
    so bringing them to true repentance
    and amendment of their lives,
for Jesus Christ's sake. **Amen.**

Prayers for the Church

34   The holy catholic Church

Most gracious Father,
we pray for your holy catholic Church:
fill it with all truth
and in all truth with all peace;
where it is corrupt, purge it;
where it is in error, direct it;
where anything is amiss, reform it;
where it is right, strengthen and confirm it;
where it is in want, furnish it;
where it is divided,
    heal it and unite it in your love;
through Jesus Christ our Lord. **Amen.**

35   Call to discipleship

Christ, whose insistent call
disturbs our settled lives:
give us discernment to hear your word,
grace to relinquish our tasks,
and courage to follow empty-handed
wherever you may lead,
so that the voice of your gospel
may reach to the ends of the earth. **Amen.**

36 Lay ministries

Almighty God, by whose Spirit the whole body of your Church
is called into a royal priesthood,
hear our prayer for all members of your Church
that in their vocation and ministry they may truly serve you,
devoutly love you and faithfully follow in the way of your Son,
Jesus Christ our Lord. **Amen.**

37 Ministry

God our Shepherd,
in every generation you call
        ministers of your word and sacraments.
Equip them to preach the gospel, to care for your people
        and to show forth the fruit of the Spirit in their lives;
in the name of Jesus our Saviour. **Amen.**

38 Those to be ordained deacon

Lord Jesus Christ,
though you are rich, for our sake you became poor.
Taking the form of a servant, you humbled yourself,
        and gave your life a ransom for many.
Send your blessing on those called to be deacons,
that they may have grace and power
        to serve as your ambassadors,
to stand beside the poor and raise up the needy,
and so proclaim your gospel of salvation in word and deed.
May they be patient and loving, strong and steadfast,
        running to the end the race set before them,
to receive your promised crown of glory. **Amen.**

39 Those to be ordained priest

Great Shepherd of your people,
bless those called to priesthood in your Church.
Fire their hearts with passion for your word
        and care for your people,
that they may joyfully proclaim your gospel,
        and faithfully minister your sacraments.

Guide them in their prayer and study,
    that they may be discerning and loving pastors,
enabling all to minister to the glory of your name
    and the benefit of your people and world.
We ask this through Jesus Christ our Lord. **Amen.**

40   At the time of choosing a Bishop

Eternal God, shepherd and guide,
in your mercy give your Church in this diocese
a shepherd after your own heart
    who will walk in your ways,
    and with loving care watch over your people.
Give us a leader of vision and a teacher of your truth.
So may your Church be built up and your name glorified;
through Jesus Christ our Lord. **Amen.**

41   At the time of choosing an incumbent

Bountiful God,
give to this parish a faithful pastor who will faithfully speak your
word and minister your sacraments;
an encourager who will equip your people for ministry
    and enable us to fulfil our calling.
Give to those who will choose, wisdom,
    discernment and patience,
    and to us give warm and generous hearts,
for Jesus Christ's sake. **Amen.**

42   Synod

Almighty and everliving God,
give wisdom and understanding,
to the members of *the Synod of this Diocese /*
    the General Synod of our Church.
Teach *them/us* in all things to seek first your honour and glory.
May *they/we* perceive what is right
  have courage to pursue it
  and grace to accomplish it,
through Jesus Christ our Lord. **Amen**

43 Before a meeting

God our Creator, when you speak there is light and life,
Fill us with your Holy Spirit
so that we may listen to one another,
speak the truth in love,
and bear much fruit in the service of your kingdom;
through Jesus Christ our Lord. **Amen.**

44 Unity

God the Father of our Lord Jesus Christ,
our only Saviour, the Prince of Peace:
give us grace seriously to lay to heart
the great danger we are in by our divisions.
Take away all prejudice and pride,
and whatever else may hinder true harmony,
for there is only one Lord, one faith, one baptism,
one God and Father of us all.
Grant that we may glorify your name together
that the world may believe in you. **Amen**

45 Unity

Lord Jesus Christ, you said to your apostles:
I leave you peace, my peace I give you.
Look not on our sins, our divisions and our confusions
   but grant us the peace and unity of your kingdom
where you live for ever and ever. **Amen.**

46 The spread of the gospel

We praise you, Lord of all,
   for the gifts of Christ our ascended King:
   for apostles, prophets, evangelists, pastors and teachers.
Hear our prayer for all who do not know your love
have not heard the gospel of our Saviour Jesus Christ.
Send out your light and truth through the messengers of your
word. Help us to support them by our prayers and offerings,
   and hasten the coming of your kingdom;
through Jesus Christ our Lord. **Amen.**

47   Mission and evangelism

O God, you have made of one blood all the peoples of the earth
and sent your Son to preach peace to those who are far off
     and to those who are near:
grant that people everywhere may seek after you and find you;
pour out your Spirit upon all flesh
and hasten the coming of your kingdom;
through Jesus Christ our Lord. **Amen**

48   The Anglican Board of Mission - Australia

God of all,
bless the Anglican Board of Mission
as it serves the Church in Australia
     and our partner churches overseas.
Inspire its work and its vision
     that all may come to know your justice,
     your peace and your love;
through Jesus Christ our Lord. **Amen.**

49   The Bush Church Aid Society

Lord our God,
we pray for all who live in remote parts of Australia.
Thank you for the Bush Church Aid Society,
     for its ministry of word and sacrament,
     its medical work and support services,
     and its care for the young.
Encourage workers in loneliness and refresh them in hardship.
Call many to stand with them in making Christ known,
that your redeeming love might be accepted
     throughout our land.
We pray in Jesus' name. **Amen.**

50   The Church Missionary Society

God of love, whose will it is that everyone should be saved,
bless the Church Missionary Society,
and all who have gone out in its fellowship
to preach, to teach and to heal.

Guard, guide and use them;
raise up more people in your worldwide Church
    to pray and to work,
    to care and to understand,
    to give to you and to go for you,
that your Church may grow, your will be done,
your kingdom come, and your glory be revealed;
through Jesus Christ our Lord. **Amen.**

Other Prayers

51   God's guidance

Almighty and everlasting God,
direct, sanctify, and govern our hearts and bodies
in the ways of your law and the works of your commandments.
By your mighty protection may we be kept safe in body and soul
and serve you with generous and joyful hearts,
bringing glory to your holy name;
through our Lord and Saviour Jesus Christ. **Amen.**

52   After hearing Holy Scripture read

God of wisdom,
grant, we pray, that the words we have heard today
may be grafted in our hearts
so that they may bring forth in us the fruit of good works
to the honour and praise of your name;
through Jesus Christ our Lord. **Amen.**

Almighty God,
we thank you for your holy word.
May it be a lantern to our feet,
    a light to our paths,
    and strength to our lives,
in the name of your Son
Jesus Christ our Lord. **Amen.**

53 For a true end

Support us, O Lord, all the day long of this troublous life,
until the shadows lengthen and the evening comes,
the busy world is hushed,
the fever of life is over,
and our work is done.
Then, Lord, in your mercy grant us a safe lodging,
a holy rest, and peace at the last;
through Christ our Lord. **Amen.**

54 Dedication

Teach us, gracious Lord,
to begin our works with reverence,
to go on in obedience,
and finish them with love;
and then to wait patiently in hope,
looking joyfully to you
whose promises are faithful and rewards infinite;
through Jesus Christ our Lord. **Amen**

55 Grace

Go before us, O Lord, in all our doings
with your most gracious favour,
and assist us with your continual help;
that in all works, begun, continued and ended in you,
we may glorify your holy name,
and finally by your mercy
obtain everlasting life;
through Jesus Christ our Lord. **Amen.**

Thanksgivings

1   A general thanksgiving

Almighty God and merciful Father,
we give you hearty thanks
for all your goodness and loving-kindness to us and to all people.
We bless you for our creation and preservation,
    and all the blessings of this life;
but above all, for your immeasurable love
in the redemption of the world by our Lord Jesus Christ,
for the means of grace, and for the hope of glory.
And, we pray, give us such a sense of all your mercies,
that our hearts may be truly thankful
and that we may praise you
not only with our lips, but in our lives,
serving you in holiness and righteousness all our days,
through Jesus Christ, our Lord,
to whom with you and the Holy Spirit, be honour and glory,
now and for ever. **Amen**

2   A general thanksgiving

Gracious God, we humbly thank you
for all your gifts so freely bestowed on us,
    for life and health and safety,
    for freedom to work and leisure to rest,
    and for all that is beautiful in creation and in human life.
But, above all, we thank you for our Saviour, Jesus Christ,
    for his death and resurrection,
    for the gift of your Spirit, and for the hope of glory.
Fill our hearts with all joy and peace in believing;
through Jesus Christ our Lord. **Amen**

3   A thanksgiving for Australia

God of holy dreaming, Great Creator Spirit,
from the dawn of creation you have given your children
   the good things of Mother Earth.
You spoke and the gum tree grew.

In the vast desert and dense forest,
and in cities at the water's edge,
creation sings your praise.
Your presence endures
as the rock at the heart of our Land.
When Jesus hung on the tree
you heard the cries of all your people
and became one with your wounded ones:
the convicts, the hunted, and the dispossessed.
The sunrise of your Son coloured the earth anew,
and bathed it in glorious hope.
In Jesus we have been reconciled to you,
to each other and to your whole creation.
Lead us on, Great Spirit,
as we gather from the four corners of the earth;
enable us to walk together in trust
from the hurt and shame of the past
into the full day which has dawned in Jesus Christ. **Amen.**

4   A litany of thanksgiving

[Let us give thanks to God, saying, 'we thank you, Lord'.]
For the beauty and wonder of creation,
   we thank you, Lord.

For all that is gracious in the lives of men and women,
   we thank you, Lord.

For daily food, for homes and families and friends,
   we thank you, Lord.

For minds to think, hearts to love, and imagination to wonder,
   we thank you, Lord.

For health, strength, and skill to work, and leisure to rest and play,
   we thank you, Lord.

For patience in suffering,
   for courage and faithfulness in difficult times,
   we thank you, Lord.

For all who pursue justice and truth,
   we thank you, Lord.

[Today we give thanks especially for...
we thank you, Lord.]

For [... and] all the saints whose lives have reflected
the light of Christ,
we thank you, Lord.

5 For the Church

Almighty God, we praise you for the blessings
brought to the world through your Church.
We bless you for the grace of the sacraments,
for our fellowship in Christ
with you and with each other,
for the teaching of the Scriptures,
and for the preaching of your word.
We thank you for the example of your saints,
for your faithful servants departed this life, and
for the memory of all that has been true and good in their lives.
Number us with them
in the company of the redeemed in heaven;
through Jesus Christ our Lord. **Amen.**

6 For the beauty of the earth

We thank you, God of all loveliness,
for the beauty of earth and sky and sea;
for the richness of mountains, deserts and rivers;
for the songs of birds and the beauty of flowers.
We praise you for these good gifts,
and pray that we may guard our heritage,
to the honour and glory of your name. **Amen**

7 For restoration of health

God of steadfast love, your mercies are new every day:
we thank you for healing *N*.
We give you thanks for the love of family and friends,
for the prayers of your people,
and for those who have ministered our healing.
Accept our thanks, through Jesus Christ our Lord. **Amen.**

Blessings

1   A blessing of the whole person

God our creator,
you have made each one of us in every part.
Bless *us* through and through,
that we may delight to serve you to the full.

Bless *our* eyes, that *we* may discern the beauty you give.
Bless *our* ears, that *we* may hear you in the music of sounds.
Bless *our* sense of smell, that your fragrance may fill *our* being.
Bless *our* lips, that *we* may speak your truth, and sing your joy.
Bless *our* hands, that they may play, write and touch
      as you guide them.
Bless *our* feet, that they may be messengers of your peace.
Bless *our* imaginations,
      that we may be fired with wonder in your truth.
Bless *our* hearts, that they may be filled with your love.

Bless *us* through and through,
that *we* may delight to serve you to the full, through Jesus Christ,
who took our nature to make us whole. **Amen.**

2   Holy eternal Majesty,
Holy incarnate Word,
Holy abiding Spirit,
Bless you for evermore. **Amen.**

3   All our problems,
      we send to the cross of Christ.
All our difficulties,
      we send to the cross of Christ.
All the devil's works,
      we send to the cross of Christ.
All our hopes,
      we set on the risen Christ.

Christ the Sun or Righteousness shine upon you
and scatter the darkness before your path; and the blessing …

Collects for Weekdays

FIRST SUNDAY IN ADVENT

Almighty God, give us grace that we may cast away the works of darkness and put on the armour of light, now in the time of this mortal life in which your Son Jesus Christ came among us in great humility, that on the last day, when he shall come again in his glorious majesty to judge the living and the dead, we may rise to the life immortal; through him who lives and reigns with you and the Holy Spirit, one God, now and for ever. **Amen.**

SECOND SUNDAY IN ADVENT

Merciful God, who sent your messenger John the Baptist to preach repentance and prepare the way for our salvation: give us grace to heed his warning and forsake our sins, that we may greet with joy the coming of our Redeemer, Jesus Christ our Lord, who lives and reigns with you and the Holy Spirit, one God, now and for ever. **Amen.**

or

O Lord Jesus Christ, who at your first coming sent your messenger to prepare your way before you: grant that the ministers and stewards of your mysteries may likewise so prepare and make ready your way by turning the hearts of the disobedient to the wisdom of the righteous, that at your second coming to judge the world we may be found an acceptable people in your sight; for you live and reign with the Father and the Holy Spirit, one God, now and for ever. **Amen.**

ANDREW 30 NOVEMBER

Everliving God, whose apostle Andrew heard the call of your Son and followed, bringing his brother with him: inspire us, like him, to offer ourselves readily for your service and to tell others the good news of your kingdom; through Jesus Christ our Lord, who lives and reigns with you and the Holy Spirit one God, now and for ever. **Amen.**

THIRD SUNDAY IN ADVENT

Almighty God, you have made us and all things to serve you: come quickly to save us, so that wars and violence shall end and your children may live in peace, honouring one another with justice and love; through Jesus Christ, your Son our Lord, who lives with you in the unity of the Holy Spirit, one God, now and for ever. **Amen.**

THOMAS 21 DECEMBER *OR 3 JULY*

Almighty and eternal God, who, for the firmer foundation of our faith, allowed the apostle Thomas to doubt the resurrection of your Son until word and sight convinced him: grant that we, who have not seen, may also believe, and so receive the fullness of your Son's blessing; who is alive and reigns with you and the Holy Spirit, one God, now and for ever. **Amen.**

FOURTH SUNDAY IN ADVENT

O Lord, raise up your power and come among us, and with great might succour us, that, whereas through our sins and wickedness we are sore let and hindered in running the race that is set before us, your bountiful grace and mercy may speedily help and deliver us; through your Son our Lord, to whom with you and the Holy Spirit be honour and glory, now and for ever. **Amen.**

CHRISTMAS

Almighty God, who gave your only-begotten Son to take our nature upon him and as at this time to be born of the virgin Mary: grant that we being born again and made your children by adoption and grace, may daily be renewed by your Holy Spirit; through the same our Lord Jesus Christ, who lives and reigns with you and the same Spirit, ever one God, now and for ever. **Amen.**

STEPHEN 26 DECEMBER *OR 3 AUGUST*

We give you thanks, O Lord of glory, for the example of Stephen, the first martyr, who prayed for his persecutors, and looked to him who was crucified, your Son Jesus Christ, who lives and reigns with you and the Holy Spirit, one God, in glory everlasting. **Amen.**

JOHN 27 DECEMBER *OR 6 MAY*

Shed upon your Church, O Lord, the brightness of your light, so that we, being illumined by the teaching of John the evangelist, may walk in the light of your truth, and be brought to the fullness of eternal life; through Jesus Christ our Lord, who lives and reigns with you and the Holy Spirit, one God, for ever and ever. **Amen.**

HOLY INNOCENTS 28 DECEMBER

Heavenly Father, whose children suffered at cruel hands, though they had done no wrong: give us grace neither to act cruelly nor to stand indifferently by, but to defend the weak from the tyranny of the strong; in the name of Jesus Christ who suffered for us, yet is alive and reigns with you and the Holy Spirit, one God, for ever and ever. **Amen.**

or

God of the dispossessed, defender of the helpless, you grieve with all the women who weep because their children are no more: may we also refuse to be comforted until the violence of the strong has been confounded, and the broken victims have been set free; in the name of Jesus Christ. **Amen.**

FIRST SUNDAY AFTER CHRISTMAS
Almighty God, you have shed upon us the light of your incarnate Word: may this light, kindled in our hearts, shine forth in our lives; through Jesus Christ our Lord, who lives and reigns with you and the Holy Spirit, one God, now and for ever. **Amen.**

SECOND SUNDAY AFTER CHRISTMAS
Almighty God, by whom the world has been filled with the light of your incarnate Word: grant, we pray, that as he kindles the flame of faith and love in our hearts so his light may shine forth in our lives; who now lives and reigns with you in the unity of the Holy Spirit, one God, for ever and ever. **Amen.**

NAMING AND CIRCUMCISION OF JESUS 1 JANUARY
God our Father, you gave to your incarnate Son the name of Jesus to be a sign of our salvation: may every tongue confess that he, who for our sake became obedient to the law, is both Lord and Christ, to your eternal glory; for he now lives and reigns with you and the Holy Spirit, one God, for ever and ever. **Amen.**

or

Christ our brother, in you there is neither Jew nor Gentile, neither male nor female, yet you received the mark of the covenant, and took upon yourself the precious burden of the law. May we so accept in our bodies our own particular struggle and promise, that we also may break down barriers, in your name. **Amen.**

EPIPHANY
O God, by the leading of a star you manifested your only-begotten Son to the Gentiles: mercifully grant, that we, who know you now by faith, may after this life be led to the vision of your glorious Godhead; through Jesus Christ our Lord. **Amen.**

PRESENTATION OF CHRIST IN THE TEMPLE 2 FEBRUARY
Almighty and everliving God, we humbly pray that, as your only Son was presented in the temple in accordance with the law, so we may be dedicated to you with pure and clean hearts; through Jesus Christ our Lord, who lives and reigns with you and the Holy Spirit, one God, now and for ever. **Amen.**

or

Christ our cornerstone,
you were recognised at your presentation in the temple
as a sign of hope for the world,
but also as a stumbling-block for many:
help us so to present ourselves for our service,
that, in sharing your scandal,
we may become a people acceptable to you.
In your name we pray. **Amen.**

BAPTISM OF THE LORD (FIRST SUNDAY AFTER EPIPHANY) [1]

Sunday between 7 and 13 January

Almighty God, who anointed Jesus at his baptism with the Holy Spirit and revealed him as your beloved Son: inspire us, your children, who are born again of water and the Spirit, to surrender our lives to your service, that we may rejoice to be called your children; through Jesus Christ our Lord. **Amen.**

SECOND SUNDAY AFTER THE EPIPHANY [2] *Sunday between 14 and 20 January*

Almighty God, by whose grace alone we are accepted and called to your service: strengthen us by your Holy Spirit and make us worthy of our calling; through Jesus Christ our Lord. **Amen.**

CONFESSION OF PETER 18 JANUARY

Almighty God, who inspired Simon Peter to confess Jesus as Messiah and Son of the living God: keep your Church steadfast upon the rock of this faith, so that in unity and peace we may proclaim the one truth and follow the one Lord, our Saviour Jesus Christ; who lives and reigns with you and the Holy Spirit, one God, now and for ever. **Amen.**

THIRD SUNDAY AFTER THE EPIPHANY [3] *Sunday between 21 and 27 January*

O God, the strength of all those who put their trust in you: mercifully accept our prayers, and because through the weakness of our mortal nature we can do nothing good without you, grant us the help of your grace, that in keeping your commandments we may please you both in will and deed; through Jesus Christ our Lord. **Amen.**

CONVERSION OF SAINT PAUL 25 JANUARY

O God, by the preaching of Paul your apostle you have caused the light of the Gospel to shine throughout the world: grant that, as we remember his wonderful conversion, we may show ourselves thankful to you by following his teaching; through Jesus Christ our Lord, who lives and reigns with you, in the unity of the Holy Spirit, one God, now and for ever. **Amen.**

AUSTRALIA DAY 26 JANUARY
Bounteous God, we give thanks for this ancient and beautiful land, a land of despair and hope, a land of wealth and abundant harvests, a land of fire, drought and flood. We pray that your Spirit may continue to move in this land and bring forgiveness, reconciliation, and an end to all injustice; through Jesus Christ our Lord. **Amen.**

FOURTH SUNDAY AFTER THE EPIPHANY [4]

Sunday between 28 January and 3 February
O Lord, you have taught us that all our doings without love are worth nothing: send your Holy Spirit, and pour into our hearts that most excellent gift of love, the true bond of peace and of all virtues, without which whoever lives is counted dead before you; Grant this for your only Son Jesus Christ's sake. **Amen.**

FIRST SERVICE IN THE COLONY OF NEW SOUTH WALES 3 FEBRUARY
Everlasting god, your messengers have carried the good news of Christ to the ends of the earth: grant that we who commemorate the builders of your Church in this land may know the truth of the gospel in our hearts and build well on the foundations they have laid; through Jesus Christ our Lord. **Amen.**

FIFTH SUNDAY AFTER THE EPIPHANY [5]

Sunday between 4 and 10 February
Father of all, who gave your only-begotten Son to take upon himself the form of a servant and to be obedient even to death on a cross: give us the same mind that was in Christ Jesus, that, sharing in his humility, we may come to be with him in his glory; where he lives and reigns with you and the Holy Spirit, one God, now and for ever. **Amen.**

SIXTH SUNDAY AFTER THE EPIPHANY [6]

Sunday between 11 and 17 February or between 8 and 14 May
Let your merciful ears, O Lord, be open to the prayers of your humble servants; and that they may obtain their petitions make them to ask such things as shall please you; through Jesus Christ our Lord. **Amen.**

SEVENTH SUNDAY AFTER THE EPIPHANY [7]

Sunday between 18 and 24 February or between 15 and 21 May
Almighty God, you have taught us through your Son that love is the fulfilling of the law: grant that we may love you with our whole heart, and our neighbours as ourselves; through Jesus Christ our Lord. **Amen.**

MATTHIAS 24 FEBRUARY

Almighty God, who chose your faithful servant Matthias to be numbered among the twelve apostles in the place of Judas: preserve your Church always from false apostles, so that it may be guided by true and faithful pastors; through Jesus Christ our Lord, who lives and reigns with you, in the unity of the Holy Spirit, one God, now and for ever. **Amen.**

EIGHTH SUNDAY AFTER THE EPIPHANY [8]

Sunday between 25 and 29 February, or

Second Sunday after Pentecost between 24 and 28 May

Grant, O Lord, that the course of this world may be so peaceably ordered by your governance, that your Church may joyfully serve you in all godly quietness; through Jesus Christ our Lord. **Amen.**

LAST SUNDAY AFTER EPIPHANY — TRANSFIGURATION

Until Ash Wednesday

Almighty God, you have given your only Son to be for us both a sacrifice for sin, and also an example of godly life: give us grace that we may always thankfully receive the benefits of his sacrifice, and also daily endeavour to follow the blessed steps of his most holy life; through the same Jesus Christ our Lord, who is alive and reigns with you and the Holy Spirit, one God, now and for ever. **Amen.**

ASH WEDNESDAY

Almighty and everlasting God, you hate nothing that you have made, and you forgive the sins of all who are penitent: create and make in us new and contrite hearts, that we, worthily lamenting our sins, and acknowledging our wretchedness, may obtain of you, the God of all mercy, perfect remission and forgiveness; through Jesus Christ our Lord. **Amen.**

FIRST SUNDAY IN LENT

O Lord, who for our sake fasted forty days and forty nights: give us grace to use such abstinence, that, our flesh being subdued to the spirit, we may ever obey your godly will in righteousness and true holiness; to your honour and glory, who live and reign with the Father and the Holy Spirit, one God, world without end. **Amen.**

SECOND SUNDAY IN LENT

Remember, O Lord, what you have wrought in us and not what we deserve, and, as you have called us to your service, make us worthy of our calling; through Jesus Christ our Lord. **Amen.**

THIRD SUNDAY IN LENT

Lord God, our Redeemer, who heard the cry of your people and sent your servant Moses to lead them out of slavery: Free us from the tyranny of sin and death and, by the leading of your Spirit, bring us to our promised land; through Jesus Christ our Lord. **Amen.**

FOURTH SUNDAY IN LENT

Almighty God, in Christ you make all things new: transform the poverty of our nature by the riches of your grace, and in the renewal of our lives make known your heavenly glory; through Jesus Christ our Lord. **Amen.**

FIFTH SUNDAY IN LENT

We thank you, heavenly Father, that you have delivered us from the power of darkness and brought us into the kingdom of your Son: we pray that as by his death he has recalled us to life, so by his presence abiding in us he may raise us to joys eternal; through Jesus Christ your Son our Lord, who lives and reigns with you in the unity of the Holy Spirit, one God, now and for ever. **Amen.**

SIXTH SUNDAY IN LENT (PASSION SUNDAY OR PALM SUNDAY)

Almighty and everlasting God, of your tender love towards us you sent your Son, our Saviour Jesus Christ, to take upon him our flesh, and to suffer death upon the cross, that all should follow the example of his great humility: mercifully grant, that we may both follow the example of his patience, and also be made partakers of his resurrection; through the same Jesus Christ our Lord. **Amen.**

MAUNDY THURSDAY

Grant, Lord, that we who receive the holy sacrament of the body and blood of our Lord Jesus Christ, may be the means by which the work of his incarnation shall go forward: take, consecrate, break and distribute us, to be for others a means of your grace, and vehicles of your eternal love; through Jesus Christ our Lord. **Amen.**

or

Holy God, source of all love, on the night of his betrayal Jesus gave his disciples a new commandment, to love one another as he loved them: write this commandment in our hearts, and give us the will to serve others as he was the servant of all, who gave his life and died for us, yet is alive and reigns with you and the Holy Spirit, one God, now and for ever. **Amen.**

or

O God, your love was embodied in Jesus Christ, who washed the disciples' feet on the night of his betrayal: wash us from the stain of sin, so that, in hours of danger, we may not fail, but follow your Son through every trial, and praise him always as Lord and Christ, to whom be glory, now and for ever. **Amen.**

GOOD FRIDAY

Lord God, whose blessed Son our Saviour gave his back to the smiters and did not hide his face from shame: give us grace to accept the sufferings of this present time with sure confidence in the glory that shall be revealed; through Jesus Christ our Lord. **Amen**.

or

Merciful God, who gave your Son to suffer the shame of the cross: save us from hardness of heart, that, seeing him who died for us, we may repent, confess our sin, and receive your overflowing love, in Jesus Christ our Lord. **Amen.**

Collects based on the Book of Common Prayer

Almighty God, look with mercy on this your family, for whom our Lord Jesus Christ was willing to be betrayed and to be given into the hands of sinners and to suffer death upon the cross; who now lives and reigns with you and the Holy Spirit, one God for ever and ever. **Amen.**

Almighty and everlasting God, by whose Spirit the whole body of the Church is governed and sanctified: receive our prayers and suppli-cations, which we offer before you for all people in your holy Church, that all its members, in their vocation and ministry, may truly and godly serve you; through our Lord and Saviour Jesus Christ. **Amen.**

O merciful God, you have made all people and you hate nothing that you have made, nor desire the death of sinners, but rather that they should turn and live: have mercy on all who have not known you, or who deny the faith of Christ crucified; take from them all ignorance, hardness of heart, and contempt of your word; and so fetch them home, blessed Lord, to your fold, that we may be made one flock under one shepherd, Jesus Christ our Lord, who lives and reigns with you and the Holy Spirit, one God, world without end. **Amen**.

HOLY SATURDAY

Grant, Lord, that as we have been baptised into the death of your dear Son, our Saviour Jesus Christ, so by continually putting to death our sinful desires we may die to sin and be buried with him, and that through the grave and gate of death we may pass to our joyful resurrection; for his sake who died, and was buried, and rose again for us, your Son, Jesus Christ our Lord. **Amen.**

or

O God, creator of heaven and earth: mercifully grant that as the crucified body of your dear Son was laid in the tomb and rested on this holy Sabbath so we may await with him the dawning of the third day, and rise with him to newness of life; who now lives and reigns with you and the Holy Spirit, one God, now and for ever. **Amen.**

EASTER

Lord of all life and power, who, through the mighty resurrection of your Son, overcame the old order of sin and death to make all things new in him: grant that we, being dead to sin and alive to you in Jesus Christ, may reign with him in glory; to whom with you and the Holy Spirit be praise, honour and thanksgiving, now and for all eternity. **Amen.**

or

Almighty God, through your only-begotten Son Jesus Christ you have overcome death and opened to us the gate of everlasting life: we humbly pray that as, by your special grace going before us, you put into our minds good desires, so by your continual help we may bring these to good effect; through Jesus Christ our Lord, who lives and reigns with you and the Holy Spirit, one God, in everlasting glory. **Amen.**

SECOND SUNDAY OF EASTER

Almighty God, whose Son Jesus Christ is the resurrection and the life of all who put their trust in him: raise us, we pray, from the death of sin to the life of righteousness; that we may ever seek the things which are above, where he reigns with you and the Holy Spirit, one God, now and for ever. **Amen.**

THIRD SUNDAY OF EASTER

Gracious Father, who in your great mercy made glad the disciples with the sight of the risen Lord: give us such awareness of his presence with us that we may be strengthened and sustained by his risen life, and serve you continually in righteousness and truth; through Jesus Christ our Lord. **Amen.**

FOURTH SUNDAY OF EASTER

God of peace, who brought again from the dead our Lord Jesus, the great shepherd of the sheep, through the blood of the everlasting covenant: make us perfect in every good work to do your will, and work in us that which is well-pleasing in your sight; through Jesus Christ our Lord. **Amen.**

or

O God, whose Son Jesus is the good shepherd of your people: Help us when we hear his voice to know him who calls us each by name, and to follow where he leads; who with you and the Holy Spirit lives and reigns, one God, for ever and ever. **Amen.**

FIFTH SUNDAY OF EASTER

Saving God, who called your Church to witness that you were in Christ reconciling the world to yourself: help us so to proclaim the good news of your love, that all who hear it may be reconciled to you; through him who died for us and rose again and reigns with you and the Holy Spirit, one God, now and for ever. **Amen.**

SIXTH SUNDAY OF EASTER

Eternal God, whose Son Jesus Christ is the way, the truth, and the life: grant that we may walk in his way, rejoice in his truth, and share his risen life; who lives and reigns with you and the Holy Spirit, one God, now and for ever. **Amen.**

ASCENSION

Grant, we pray, almighty God,
that as we believe your only Son, our Lord Jesus Christ, to have ascended into the heavens, so we may also in heart and mind thither ascend, and with him continually dwell; who lives and reigns with you and the Holy Spirit, one God, in glory everlasting. **Amen.**

or

Almighty God, your Son Jesus Christ ascended to the throne of heaven that he might rule over all things as Lord: keep the Church in the unity of the Spirit and in the bond of peace; and bring all creation to worship at his feet, who is alive and reigns with you and the Holy Spirit, one God, now and for ever. **Amen.**

SEVENTH SUNDAY OF EASTER

O God, the King of glory, you have exalted your only Son Jesus Christ with great triumph to your kingdom in heaven: we pray you, leave us not comfortless, but send your Holy Spirit to strengthen us, and exalt us to the same place where our Saviour Christ has gone before; who lives and reigns with you and the Holy Spirit, one God, for ever and ever. **Amen.**

or

O God, you withdraw from our sight that you may be known by our love: help us to enter the cloud where you are hidden, and to surrender all our certainty to the darkness of faith in Jesus Christ. **Amen.**

DAY OF PENTECOST

See the prayer for the appropriate Sunday after Epiphany or Pentecost

TRINITY SUNDAY

Almighty and everlasting God, you have given to us your servants grace by the confession of a true faith to acknowledge the glory of the eternal Trinity, and in the power of the divine majesty to worship the Unity: keep us steadfast in this faith, and evermore defend us from all adversities, for you live and reign, one God, for ever and ever. **Amen.**

THE ANNUNCIATION TO THE BLESSED VIRGIN MARY 25 MARCH

We beseech you, O Lord, pour your grace into our hearts, that, as we have known the incarnation of your Son Jesus Christ by the message of an angel, so by his cross and passion we may be brought to the glory of his resurrection; who lives and reigns with you in the unity of the Holy Spirit, one God, now and for ever. **Amen.**

MARK 25 (OR 26) APRIL

Almighty God, by the inspired witness of Mark the evangelist you have given to your Church the gospel of Jesus Christ your Son: strengthen us by this saving message that we may not be carried away with every changing wind of doctrine but be firmly grounded in the truth of your word; through Jesus Christ our Lord, who lives and reigns with you and the Holy Spirit, one God, for ever and ever. **Amen.**

ANZAC DAY 25 APRIL

O God, our ruler and guide, in whose hands are the destinies of this and every nation, we give you thanks for the freedoms we enjoy in this land, and for those who laid down their lives to defend them:
We pray that we and all the people of Australia, gratefully remembering their courage and their sacrifice, may have grace to live in a spirit of justice, of generosity, and of peace; through Jesus Christ our Lord, who lives and reigns with you and the Holy Spirit, one God, for ever and ever. **Amen.**

PHILIP AND JAMES 1 MAY

Almighty God, whom truly to know is eternal life: teach us to know your Son Jesus Christ to be the way, the truth, and the life, so that, following in the steps of your apostles Philip and James, we may steadfastly walk in the way that leads to eternal life; through Jesus Christ your Son our Lord. **Amen.**

SUNDAY BETWEEN 29 MAY AND 4 JUNE [9] *other than Trinity Sunday*
Almighty and everliving God, increase in us your gift of faith, so that, forsaking what lies behind and reaching out to that which is before us, we may run the way of your commandments and win the crown of everlasting joy; through Jesus Christ our Lord. **Amen.**

THE VISIT OF THE BLESSED VIRGIN MARY TO ELIZABETH 31 MAY
Father in heaven, by whose grace Mary was blessed among women in bearing your incarnate Son, and still more blessed in believing your promises and in keeping your word: help us, who honour the exaltation of her lowliness, to follow her in obeying your will; through Jesus Christ our Lord, who lives and reigns with you and the Holy Spirit, one God, for ever and ever. **Amen.**

or

O God our deliverer, you cast down the mighty, and lift up those of no account: as Elizabeth and Mary embrace1d with songs of liberation, so may we also be pregnant with your Spirit, and affirm one another in hope for the world; through Jesus Christ. **Amen.**

SUNDAY BETWEEN 5 AND 11 JUNE [10]
O Lord, from whom alone all good things come: grant that by your holy inspiration we may think those things that are good, and by your merciful guiding may perform them; through our Lord Jesus Christ. **Amen**.

BARNABAS 11 JUNE
Generous God, whose Son Jesus Christ has taught us that it is more blessed to give than to receive: help us by the example of your apostle Barnabas, a good man, full of the Holy Spirit and of faith, to be generous in our judgements and unselfish in our service; through Jesus Christ our Lord, who lives and reigns with you and the Holy Spirit, one God, for ever and ever. **Amen.**

SUNDAY BETWEEN 12 AND 18 JUNE [11]
Lord, we beseech you to keep your family, the Church, in continual godliness, that through your protection it may be free from all adversities, and devoutly given to serve you in good works, to the glory of your name; through Jesus Christ our Lord. **Amen.**

SUNDAY BETWEEN 19 AND 25 JUNE [12]

Almighty and everlasting God, you are always more ready to hear than we to pray, and give more than either we desire or deserve: pour down upon us the abundance of your mercy, forgiving us those things of which our conscience is afraid, and giving us those good things which we are not worthy to ask, save through the merits and mediation of Jesus Christ, your Son our Lord. **Amen.**

BIRTH OF JOHN THE BAPTIST 24 JUNE

Almighty God, by whose providence your servant John the Baptist was wonderfully born, and sent to prepare the way for your Son our Saviour by preaching a baptism of repentance: make us so to follow his teaching and holy life, that we may truly repent, and, following his example, may constantly speak the truth, boldly rebuke vice, and patiently suffer for the truth's sake; through Jesus Christ your Son our Lord, who lives and reigns with you and the Holy Spirit, one God, for ever and ever. **Amen.**

THE COMING OF THE LIGHT 1 JULY

Almighty God, you have given to the people of the Islands of the Torres Strait the glorious light of the Gospel of Christ: mercifully grant that we may always walk in the light of his love, and give us the strength and unifying power of your Holy Spirit to spread that light and enlarge your kingdom in the hearts of all people. We ask this through our Lord Jesus Christ, your Son, who lives and reigns with you and the Holy Spirit, one God, for ever and ever. **Amen.**

SUNDAY BETWEEN 26 JUNE AND 2 JULY [13]

O God, who for our redemption gave your only-begotten Son to suffer death upon a cross, and by his glorious resurrection delivered us from the power of the enemy: grant us so to die daily to sin that we may evermore live with him in the joy of his resurrection; through the same Jesus Christ our Lord. **Amen.**

PETER AND PAUL 29 JUNE

Almighty God, whose apostles Peter and Paul glorified you in their deaths as in their lives: grant that your Church, inspired by their teaching and example, and knit together in unity by your Spirit, may ever stand firm upon the one foundation, your Son Jesus Christ our Lord; who lives and reigns with you, in the unity of the Holy Spirit, one God, now and for ever. **Amen.**

or (to commemorate Peter)

Almighty God, who by your Son Jesus Christ gave your apostle Peter many excellent gifts, and commanded him earnestly to feed your flock: enable, we pray, all bishops and pastors diligently to preach your holy word, and your people faithfully to follow it, that they may receive the crown of everlasting life; through Jesus Christ our Lord. **Amen.**

SUNDAY BETWEEN 3 AND 9 JULY [14]

O God, you have prepared for those who love you such good things as pass our understanding: pour into our hearts such love toward you, that, loving you above all things, we may obtain your promises which exceed all that we can desire; through Jesus Christ our Lord. **Amen.**

SUNDAY BETWEEN 10 AND 16 JULY [15]

O Lord, we beseech you mercifully to receive the prayers of your people who call upon you, and grant that they may both perceive and know what things they ought to do, and also may have grace and power faithfully to fulfil them; through Jesus Christ our Lord. **Amen.**

SUNDAY BETWEEN 17 AND 23 JULY [16]

O God, you alone can order our unruly wills and affections: teach us to love what you command, and to desire what you promise, that, among the changes and chances of this world, our hearts may surely there be fixed where true joys are to be found; through Christ our Lord. **Amen.**

MARY MAGDALENE 22 JULY

Almighty God, whose Son called Mary Magdalene to be a witness of his resurrection: mercifully grant that by your grace we may be forgiven and healed, and may know you in the power of your Son's risen life; who with you and the Holy Spirit lives and reigns, one God, now and for ever. **Amen.**

or

Christ our healer, beloved and remembered by women, speak to the grief that makes us forget, and the terror that makes us cling, and give us back our name, so that we may greet you clearly, and proclaim your risen life. **Amen.**

SUNDAY BETWEEN 24 AND 30 JULY [17]

O God, the protector of all that trust in you, without whom nothing is strong, nothing is holy: increase and multiply upon us your mercy, that, with you as our ruler and guide, we may so pass through things temporal that we finally lose not the things eternal. Grant this, O heavenly Father, for the sake of Jesus Christ, our Lord. **Amen.**

JAMES THE APOSTLE 25 JULY

O gracious God, whose apostle James left his father and all that he had, and without delay obeyed the call of your Son Jesus Christ: pour out upon the leaders of your Church the same spirit of self-denying service by which alone they may have true authority among your people; through Jesus Christ our Lord, who lives and reigns with you and the Holy Spirit, one God, now and for ever. **Amen.**

SUNDAY BETWEEN 31 JULY AND 6 AUGUST [18]

Almighty God, whose beloved Son for our sake willingly endured the agony and shame of the cross: give us courage and patience to take up our cross daily and follow him; who lives and reigns with you and the Holy Spirit, one God, now and for ever. **Amen.**

TRANSFIGURATION OF OUR LORD 6 AUGUST

Eternal God, our glorious King, whose Son Jesus Christ was transfigured on the holy mountain and seen in splendour by his chosen witnesses: grant us, his followers, faith to perceive his glory, to listen to him, and to walk in his way, that we may be changed into his likeness from glory to glory; for he lives and reigns with you and the Holy Spirit, one God, for ever and ever. **Amen.**

SUNDAY BETWEEN 7 AND 13 AUGUST [19]

Grant to us, Lord, we beseech you,
the spirit to think and do always such things as are right,
that we, who cannot do anything that is good without you,
may by you be enabled to live according to your will;
through Jesus Christ our Lord. **Amen.**

SUNDAY BETWEEN 14 AND 20 AUGUST [20]

Almighty God, you have given your only Son to be for us both a sacrifice for sin and also an example of godly life: give us grace that we may always thankfully receive the benefits of his sacrifice, and also daily endeavour to follow the blessed steps of his most holy life; through the same Jesus Christ our Lord. **Amen.**

MARY, MOTHER OF OUR LORD 15 AUGUST

Loving God, who chose the blessed virgin Mary to be the mother of your incarnate Son: grant that we, who are redeemed by his blood, may share with her in the glory of your eternal kingdom; through Jesus Christ our Lord, who lives and reigns with you, in the unity of the Holy Spirit, one God, now and for ever. **Amen.**

or

Heavenly Father, who chose the virgin Mary, by your grace, to be the mother of our Lord and Saviour: fill us with your grace, that in all things we may accept your holy will and with her rejoice in your salvation; through Jesus Christ our Lord. **Amen.**

SUNDAY BETWEEN 21 AND 27 AUGUST [21]

Creator God, you have made us for yourself, and our hearts are restless until they find their rest in you: teach us to offer ourselves to your service, that here we may have your peace, and in the world to come may see you face to face; through Jesus Christ our Lord. **Amen.**

BARTHOLOMEW 24 AUGUST

Almighty and everlasting God, who gave to your apostle Bartholomew grace to believe and to preach your word: grant that your Church may love that word which he believed and may faithfully receive and boldly preach it; through Jesus Christ our Lord, who lives and reigns with you and the Holy Spirit, one God, for ever and ever. **Amen.**

SUNDAY BETWEEN 28 AUGUST AND 3 SEPTEMBER [22]

Lord of all power and might,
the author and giver of all good things:
graft in our hearts the love of your name,
increase in us true religion,
nourish us with all goodness,
and of your great mercy keep us in the same;
through Jesus Christ our Lord. **Amen.**

MARTYRS OF NEW GUINEA 2 SEPTEMBER

All powerful and everliving God,
turn our weakness into strength:
as you gave the martyrs of Papua–New Guinea
the courage to suffer death for Christ,
give us the courage to live in faithful witness to you.
We ask this through Jesus Christ our Lord. **Amen.**

or

Living God, you made your Church to grow through the zeal, courage, and unflinching witness of your servants martyred in New Guinea: give to us and all your people such steadfast faith in your good purposes that we may serve faithfully wherever you have stationed us; through Jesus Christ our Lord. **Amen.**

SUNDAY BETWEEN 4 AND 10 SEPTEMBER [23]

O God, you know us to be set in the midst of so many and so great dangers that by reason of the frailty of our nature we cannot always stand upright: grant to us such strength and protection as may support us in all dangers and carry us through all temptations; through Jesus Christ our Lord. **Amen.**

SUNDAY BETWEEN 11 AND 17 SEPTEMBER [24]

O God, without you we are not able to please you: mercifully grant that your Holy Spirit may in all things direct and rule our hearts; through Jesus Christ our Lord. **Amen.**

HOLY CROSS 14 SEPTEMBER

Loving God, whose Son our Saviour Jesus Christ was lifted high upon the cross so that he might draw all people to himself: mercifully grant to us, who glory in the mystery of our redemption, the grace to take up our cross daily and follow him; who lives and reigns with you and the Holy Spirit, one God, in glory everlasting. **Amen.**

SUNDAY BETWEEN 18 AND 24 SEPTEMBER [25]

Loving Father, whose Son Jesus Christ has taught us that what we do for the least of our brothers and sisters we do also for him: give us the will to be the servant of others as he was the servant of all, who gave up his life and died for us, and yet lives and reigns with you and the Holy Spirit, one God, now and for ever. **Amen.**

MATTHEW 21 SEPTEMBER

Almighty God, who through your Son Jesus Christ called Matthew from the selfish pursuit of gain to become an apostle and evangelist: free us from all greed and love of riches so that we may follow the steps of our Lord Jesus Christ in the way of self-giving love; who lives and reigns with you and the Holy Spirit, one God, now and for ever. **Amen.**

SUNDAY BETWEEN 25 SEPTEMBER AND 1 OCTOBER [26]

O God, you declare your almighty power chiefly in showing mercy and pity: mercifully grant us such a measure of your grace that, running in the way of your commandments, we may obtain your gracious promises, and be made partakers of your heavenly treasure; through Jesus Christ our Lord. **Amen.**

MICHAEL AND ALL ANGELS 29 SEPTEMBER

Almighty God, you govern the courses of this world by means too wonderful for us to comprehend: give us reverence before the mysteries of your providence, and grace to know the messengers of your will; through Jesus Christ our Lord. **Amen.**

or

Everlasting God, you have ordained and constituted in a wonderful order the ministries of angels and mortals: grant that, as your holy angels stand before you in heaven, so at your command they may help and defend us here on earth; through Jesus Christ our Lord, who lives and reigns with you and the Holy Spirit, one God, now and for ever. **Amen.**

SUNDAY BETWEEN 2 AND 8 OCTOBER [27]

Generous God, whose hand is open to fill all things living with plenteousness: make us ever thankful for your goodness, and grant that we, remembering the account that we must one day give, may be faithful stewards of your bounty; through Jesus Christ our Lord. **Amen.**

SUNDAY BETWEEN 9 AND 15 OCTOBER [28]

Almighty God, in your wisdom you have so ordered our earthly life that we must walk by faith and not by sight: give us such trust in your fatherly care that in the face of all perplexities we may give proof of our faith by the courage of our lives; through Jesus Christ our Lord. **Amen.**

SUNDAY BETWEEN 16 AND 22 OCTOBER [29]

Almighty God, your Son has opened for us a new and living way into your presence: give us pure hearts and steadfast wills to worship you in spirit and in truth; through the same Jesus Christ our Lord. **Amen.**

LUKE 18 OCTOBER

Almighty God, who inspired your servant Luke the physician to set forth in his Gospel the love and healing power of your Son: graciously continue in your Church this love and power to heal, to the praise and glory of your name; through Jesus Christ our Lord, who lives and reigns with you, in the unity of the Holy Spirit, one God, now and for ever. **Amen.**

or

Gracious and loving God, you chose Luke the evangelist to reveal in his Gospel the mystery of your love for the poor and outcast: unite in heart and spirit all who profess your name, and lead all nations to seek your salvation in Jesus Christ, your Son; who lives and reigns with you and the Holy Spirit, one God, for ever and ever. **Amen.**

SUNDAY BETWEEN 23 AND 29 OCTOBER [30]

Almighty and everlasting God, give to us the increase of faith, hope and love; and, that we may obtain what you promise, make us to love what you command; through Jesus Christ our Lord. **Amen.**

SIMON AND JUDE 28 OCTOBER

Almighty God, you have built your Church on the foundation of the apostles and prophets, with Jesus Christ himself as the chief cornerstone: we thank you for the apostles Simon and Jude, and we pray that we may reveal your love and mercy, and being joined in unity of spirit may grow into a holy temple, acceptable to you; through our Lord and Saviour Jesus Christ, who lives and reigns with you and the Holy Spirit, one God, for ever and ever. **Amen.**

SUNDAY BETWEEN 30 OCTOBER AND 5 NOVEMBER [31]

God our Father, whose will it is to bring all things to order and unity in our Lord Jesus Christ: may all the peoples of the world, now divided and torn apart by sin, be brought together under his sovereign rule of love; through Jesus Christ our Lord. **Amen.**

ALL SAINTS 1 NOVEMBER *or first Sunday in November*

We praise you, heavenly Father, that you have knit together your chosen ones in one communion and fellowship in the body of your Son, Jesus Christ our Lord: give us grace so to follow your blessed saints in all virtuous and godly living that we may come to those inexpressible joys you have prepared for those who truly love you; through Jesus Christ our Saviour, who with you and the Holy Spirit lives and reigns, one God, in glory everlasting. **Amen.**

or

Eternal God, neither death nor life can separate us from your love: grant that we may serve you faithfully here on earth, and in heaven rejoice with all your saints who ceaselessly proclaim your glory; through Jesus Christ our Lord, who lives and reigns with you and the Holy Spirit, one God, for ever and ever. **Amen.**

ALL SOULS 2 NOVEMBER

We thank you, loving God, for all your servants, known to us and unknown, who have departed this life in your faith and fear: give us grace so to follow their good examples, that with them we may be brought to a joyful resurrection, and be made partakers of your heavenly kingdom; through Jesus Christ our Lord, who lives and reigns with you and the Holy Spirit, one God, for ever and ever. **Amen.**

SUNDAY BETWEEN 6 AND 12 NOVEMBER [32]

Blessed Lord, you have caused all holy Scriptures to be written for our learning: grant that we may so hear them, read, mark, learn and inwardly digest them, that, by patience and the comfort of your holy word, we may embrace and ever hold fast the blessed hope of everlasting life, which you have given us in our Saviour Jesus Christ. **Amen.**

SUNDAY BETWEEN 13 AND 19 NOVEMBER [33]

Almighty God, whose sovereign purpose none can make void: give us faith to be steadfast amid the tumults of this world, knowing that your kingdom shall come and your will be done, to your eternal glory; through Jesus Christ our Lord, who lives and reigns with you and the Holy Spirit, one God, now and for ever. **Amen.**

SUNDAY BETWEEN 20 AND 26 NOVEMBER [34]
(CHRIST THE KING / THE REIGN OF CHRIST)

Stir up, we pray you, O Lord, the wills of your faithful people, that they, plenteously bringing forth the fruit of good works, may by you be plenteously rewarded; through Jesus Christ our Lord. **Amen.**

DEDICATION FESTIVAL

Bountiful God, to whose glory we celebrate the dedication of this house of prayer: we praise you for the many blessings you have given to those who worship here, and we pray that all who seek you in this place may find you, and being filled with the Holy Spirit may become a living temple acceptable to you, through Jesus Christ our Lord. **Amen.**

ROGATION DAYS AND HARVEST FESTIVALS

Bountiful God, you crown the year with your goodness and give us the fruits of the earth in due season: give us grateful hearts that we may sincerely thank you for all your loving kindness, and truly care for your creation; through Jesus Christ, our Lord. **Amen.**

EMBER DAYS

Almighty God, the giver of all good gifts, by your Holy Spirit you have appointed various orders of ministry in your Church: look with mercy and favour on all who are called to serve you in the sacred ministry, that they may faithfully serve you to the glory of your name and the benefit of your Church and people; through Jesus Christ our Lord, who lives and reigns with you in the unity of the Holy Spirit, one God, now and for ever. **Amen.**

THANKSGIVING FOR THE HOLY COMMUNION

The Thursday after Trinity Sunday and other occasions

O God, in a wonderful sacrament you have given us a memorial of the passion of your dear Son: grant that we may so reverence the sacred mysteries of his body and blood that we may ever know within ourselves the fruits of his redemption; who is alive and reigns with you and the Holy Spirit, one God, now and for ever. **Amen.**

THANKSGIVING FOR HOLY BAPTISM

God of life, who anointed Jesus at his baptism with the Holy Spirit and revealed him as your beloved Son: inspire us, who in baptism are born of water and the Spirit, to surrender our lives to your service and to rejoice to be called your children; through Jesus Christ our Lord. **Amen.**

FOR THE UNITY OF CHRISTIANS

O God, whose Son Jesus Christ said to his apostles, Peace I leave with you, my peace I give to you: regard not our sins but the faith of your Church, and grant it that peace and unity that is agreeable to your will; through Jesus Christ our Lord. **Amen.**

A MARTYR

Almighty God, who gave to your servant N boldness to confess the name of Jesus Christ and courage to die for this faith: teach us always to be ready to give a reason for the hope that is in us, and to suffer gladly for the sake of our Lord and Saviour; who lives and reigns with you and the Holy Spirit, one God, for ever and ever. **Amen.**

or

Almighty God, by whose grace and power your holy martyr N triumphed over suffering and was faithful even to death: grant that we, who now remember her in thanksgiving, may be so faithful in our witness to you in this world, that we may receive with her the crown of everlasting life; through Jesus Christ our Lord, who lives and reigns with you and the Holy Spirit, one God, for ever and ever. **Amen.**

A MISSIONARY

Almighty and everlasting God, we thank you for your servant N, whom you called to bring the gospel to the people of…(*to the…people*): raise up in this and every land evangelists and heralds of your loving reign, so that the whole world may know the unsearchable riches of our Saviour Jesus Christ; who lives and reigns with you and the Holy Spirit, one God, now and for ever. **Amen.**

A PASTOR

Heavenly Father, loving shepherd of your people, we thank you for your servant N, who was faithful in the care and nurture of your flock; and we pray that, we may follow the good of his example and grow into the fullness of the stature of our Lord and Saviour Jesus Christ; who lives and reigns with you and the Holy Spirit, one God, for ever and ever. **Amen.**

A BISHOP

O God, our heavenly Father, who raised up your faithful servant N to be a bishop in your Church and to feed your flock: give abundantly to all bishops and other pastors the gifts of your Holy Spirit, so that they may minister in your household as true servants of Christ and stewards of your holy mysteries; through Jesus Christ our Lord, who lives and reigns with you and the Holy Spirit, one God, for ever and ever. **Amen.**

A THEOLOGIAN OR TEACHER

Almighty God, who gave to your servant N special gifts of grace to understand and teach the truth in Christ Jesus: grant that, enlightened by this teaching, we may know you, the one true God, and Jesus Christ whom you have sent; who lives and reigns with you and the Holy Spirit, one God, for ever and ever. **Amen.**

A MONASTIC OR ASCETIC

O God, whose blessed Son became poor so that we through his poverty might become rich: deliver us from an inordinate love of this world, so that, inspired by the devotion of your servant N, we may serve you with singleness of heart, and attain to the riches of the age to come; through Jesus Christ our Lord, who lives and reigns with you, in the unity of the Holy Spirit, one God, now and for ever. **Amen.**

A SAINT

Faithful God, you have surrounded us with a great cloud of witnesses: grant that we, encouraged by the example of your servant N, may persevere in running the race that is set before us, until at last with him we may attain to your eternal joy; through Jesus Christ, the pioneer and perfecter of our faith, who lives and reigns with you and the Holy Spirit, one God, for ever and ever. **Amen.**

or

O God, by whose grace your servant *N* became a burning and a shining light in your Church: grant that we also may be aflame with the spirit of love and discipleship, and walk before you as children of light; through Jesus Christ our Lord, who lives and reigns with you, in the unity of the Holy Spirit, one God, now and for ever. **Amen.**

My Prayers and Notes

My Prayers and Notes

My Prayers and Notes

My Prayers and Notes